Cambridge Elements ≡

Elements in Business Strategy
edited by
J.-C. Spender
Kozminski University

KNOWLEDGE STRATEGIES

Constantin Bratianu
Bucharest University of Economic Studies

CAMBRIDGE
UNIVERSITY PRESS

CAMBRIDGE
UNIVERSITY PRESS

University Printing House, Cambridge CB2 8BS, United Kingdom

One Liberty Plaza, 20th Floor, New York, NY 10006, USA

477 Williamstown Road, Port Melbourne, VIC 3207, Australia

314–321, 3rd Floor, Plot 3, Splendor Forum, Jasola District Centre, New Delhi – 110025, India

103 Penang Road, #05–06/07, Visioncrest Commercial, Singapore 238467

Cambridge University Press is part of the University of Cambridge.

It furthers the University's mission by disseminating knowledge in the pursuit of education, learning, and research at the highest international levels of excellence.

www.cambridge.org
Information on this title: www.cambridge.org/9781108818858
DOI: 10.1017/9781108864237

© Constantin Bratianu 2022

First published 2022

A catalogue record for this publication is available from the British Library.

ISBN 978-1-108-81885-8 Paperback
ISSN 2515-0693 (online)
ISSN 2515-0685 (print)

Knowledge Strategies

Elements in Business Strategy

DOI: 10.1017/9781108864237
First published online: July 2022

Constantin Bratianu
Bucharest University of Economic Studies
Author for correspondence: Constantin Bratianu, constantin.bratianu@gmail.com

Abstract: Knowledge is a strategic resource for any organization and its deployment is critical in achieving a sustainable competitive advantage. Knowledge strategies were born at the intersection of strategic thinking and knowledge management. Strategic thinking is a mental process of understanding the future and, based on that understanding, of searching for practical ways to achieve a competitive advantage in the market. Strategic thinking is operating in the opportunity space of the organization. This Element explains the strategizing process and presents the knowledge strategies which result from that complex mental process. Organizations can design deliberate and emergent knowledge strategies, which can be integrated into the corporate vision and its strategies.

Keywords: knowledge management, knowledge strategies, knowledge creation, knowledge acquisition, knowledge sharing

ISBNs: 9781108818858 (PB), 9781108864237 (OC)
ISSNs: 2515-0693 (online), 2515-0685 (print)

Contents

1 Introduction

Knowledge strategies were born at the intersection of strategic thinking and knowledge management. Strategic thinking is a mental process of understanding the future and, based on that understanding, of searching for practical ways of achieving a competitive advantage in the market. Strategic thinking is operating in the *opportunity space*, which is "the company's market potential given its environment, including such factors as the demand for its products, the cost and availability of inputs, and the legal and legislative climate" (Spender & Strong, 2014, p. 10). Strategic thinking integrates the company's business model into time perception and identifies the key uncertainties for which solutions should be found.

Knowledge management is a complex process that integrates knowledge creation and acquisition; knowledge sharing and transfer; knowledge transformation, storage, and retrieval; knowledge risks; and knowledge application in creating products and services (Jashapara, 2011; Nonaka & Takeuchi, 1995; North & Kumta, 2018). Managing knowledge is incomparably more difficult than managing tangible resources because of its conceptual nature and nonlinearity. Being intangible, knowledge cannot be seen, cannot be touched, and cannot be measured by the metrics designed for tangible objects. However, knowledge is one of the key strategic resources for many companies, and its strategic management is essential for achieving a competitive advantage for the company (Donate & Canales, 2012; Spender & Grant, 1996; Zack, 2003). In Zack's view, *knowledge strategy* can be "thought of as balancing knowledge-based resources and capabilities to the knowledge required for providing products or services in ways superior to those of competitors" (Zack, 1999, p. 131).

Strategic thinking is about the future, but the future does not exist in our daily experience. It exists only in our minds and only within the framework of our perception of time and its dynamics. Because that perception depends on our experience and cultural context, the strategic thinking paradigm will not be the same for all managers, although the basic ingredients remain the same. These ingredients are uncertainty and the absence of knowledge. Both uncertainty and absence of knowledge increase with distance from the present time, making *strategic work* (Spender, 2014) more difficult. Logical thinking designed for a state of certainty cannot provide solutions for such a future. It must be integrated with imagination and creativity to yield better support for *strategizing*. Paraphrasing Descartes, Nonaka and Zhu (2012, p. 136) assert, "We strategize; therefore we are." Thus, strategizing is a necessity for exploring the future because it is uncertain. "No uncertainties, no strategic work, no innovative activity, no learning experience" (Spender, 2014, p. 28).

Zack (1999) emphasizes the need to be aware of the *strategic gap*, which comes from a *knowledge gap* between *known* and *unknown*, between what the organization knows about its current situation and where the company intends to be. This knowledge gap requires the company to design strategies to reduce the magnitude of that gap. As Zack (1999, p. 135) underscores, "Having performed a strategic evaluation of its knowledge-based resources and capabilities, an organization can determine which knowledge should be developed or acquired. To give knowledge management a strategic focus, the firm's knowledge management initiatives should be directed toward closing this strategic knowledge gap."

Using this as our starting point, we analyze basic knowledge strategies from two opposing metaphorical perspectives: a) time is stationary, and the observer is moving toward the future, and b) the observer is stationary and time is flying toward him or her. The first perspective requires deliberate strategies, while the second perspective needs emergent strategies. However, knowledge strategies are integrated strategies that contain both deliberate and emergent components.

Unpacking the dynamic of the *known-unknowns* (Dalkir, 2005; Rumsfeld, 2002), we identify four generic knowledge strategies that are available to any company: knowledge exploitation, knowledge acquisition, knowledge sharing, and knowledge exploration. These strategies can be used alone or they can be combined to generate knowledge synergy. The state of organizational knowledge that is the most complex and difficult to understand is represented by *unknown-unknowns*, which reflect the dynamics of uncertainty and the absence of knowledge that is unpredictable. Knowledge exploration can be the designed strategy, but it must be supported by visionary leadership and creative organizational culture.

Emergent strategies aim to enhance organizational learning and develop learning organizations. These strategies integrate a conceptual design with practical implementation to provide a faster answer to the need for emergent knowledge. Smart companies develop integrated designs, which contain both deliberate and emergent knowledge strategies (Bolisani & Bratianu, 2018).

2 Understanding the Future

2.1 The Complexity of Time and Its Perception

Time is an abstract concept, and its understanding is based on our metaphorical thinking. Since our experience is influenced by events and motion in space, the main properties of the concept of time are consequences of the properties of events: "Time is directional and irreversible because events are directional and irreversible; events cannot 'unhappen.' Time is continuous because we experience events as continuous. Time is segmentable because periodic events have beginnings and ends. Time can be measured because iterations of events can be counted" (Lakoff & Johnson, 1999, p. 138). In conclusion, time is linear and irreversible.

Metaphorical thinking is a cognitive process of understanding abstract concepts by analogy with known objects from the external world (Fauconnier & Turner, 2002; Lakoff & Johnson, 1980; Pinker, 2008). A metaphor is a conceptual construct composed of two semantic domains and a mapping function. The *source* domain contains the known object and its attributes, while the *target* domain contains the abstract concept and its potential attributes. Based on our experience and judgment, we use the *mapping function* to transfer some attributes of the known object from the source domain to the abstract concept from the target domain. Thus, an abstract concept reflects the structure and some features of the known entity. For instance, in the "time is money" metaphor, we have money in the source domain and time in the target domain. Then, attributes of money like saving, wasting, and budgeting can be mapped onto the target domain and enrich the concept of time (Lakoff & Johnson, 1999). Thus, *time* becomes an economic resource that can be used to measure and improve work efficiency (Drucker, 1993; Stiglitz & Walsh, 2002). A metaphor is a semantic construct that is unidirectional and asymmetric. It is *unidirectional* because the mapping function acts only from the source domain to the target domain. It is *asymmetric* because the target domain has a deficit of attributes for the abstract concept – a deficit we want to reduce by using the mapping function. Not all the attributes from the source domain can be mapped onto the target domain, and not all the attributes in the target domain originate in the source domain. For *time*, the most important metaphors are based on comparisons with *space* and *motion*. We understand time through spatial metaphors (Boroditsky, 2000; Lakoff & Johnson, 1999).

For most people, especially those from a European or American culture, orientation in time emerges from their orientation in space. Imagine yourself standing up and looking straight in front of you for the next destination. That is mapped in the time domain as being positioned in the *present* and looking forward to the *future*. Behind you is the road already traveled, which is mapped in the time domain as being your *past*. As Núñez and Sweetser remark (2006, p. 402), "all documented languages (with the exception to be discussed later) appear to share a spatial metaphor mapping future events onto spatial locations in front of Ego and past events onto locations behind Ego." Thus, the structure of the *time orientation* metaphor can be represented as follows (Lakoff & Johnson, 1999, p. 140):

> The position of the observer ≫ The present
> The space in front of the observer ≫ The future
> The space behind the observer ≫ The past

The Aymara language and culture make an exception to this time orientation. Aymara is an Amerindian language spoken by people living in western Bolivia, southeastern Peru, and northern Chile. "In Aymara, the basic word for FRONT (*nayra*, 'eye/front/sight') is also a basic expression meaning PAST, and the basic word for BACK (*qhipa*, 'back/behind') is a basic expression for FUTURE meaning" (Núñez & Sweetser, 2006, p. 402). The logic supporting this interpretation comes from the fact that the future cannot be seen, and thus it should be placed behind us, while the past is known and can be placed in front of us.

The time orientation metaphor uses space in the source domain, but it says nothing about motion. It is a static metaphor. In a dynamic perspective, we may consider that between the observer and time, there is motion. We may have a *moving observer (moving Ego)* metaphor or a *moving time* metaphor. In the first metaphor, time is motionless, like the landscape in which the observer is moving. Consider yourself driving a car on a highway. Each location you pass is a time event. Your destination is somewhere in the future, which is in front of you. In this metaphor, we travel in the time domain from the present location toward a future one, and events may be short or long. We express this motion through the time landscape by using sentences like:

> Will your visit be a *short* or a *long* one?
> That conference runs *from* the 25th *to* the 29th of October.
> She is *halfway through* her project.

Also, in sports, the tradition is to indicate the start of a competition by saying: one, two, three, go! That time sequence leads to the starting moment of the competition, which means the initiation of a spatial sequence.

In the moving time metaphor, the observer is stationary and facing in a fixed direction. "There is an indefinitely long sequence of objects moving past the observer from front to back. The moving objects are conceptualized as having fronts in their direction of motion" (Lakoff & Johnson, 1999, p. 141). Time is flying toward the observer, and events are associated with the moving objects. We express this moving time by using sentences like:

> The Christmas holiday is *coming* upon us.
> Time is *flying by.*
> The deadline for submitting papers *has passed.*

Following this metaphor, starting a special event like launching a rocket uses the countdown: five, four, three, two, one, zero! It is really interesting to compare these two metaphors to understand how time influences our decision-making. The *moving observer* metaphor applies mostly to deliberate strategies, while the *moving time* metaphor applies mostly to emergent strategies.

Time perception is also related to motion along a lateral direction – that is, the left–right axis (Casasanto & Jasmin, 2012; Ouellet et al., 2010; Santiago et al., 2007). The lateral axis is used to show the direction of writing and reading: from left to right or from right to left. Thus, the lateral axis is also a connection between culture and the perception of time. In a famous experiment, children and adults of European and American cultures were asked to arrange three stickers with the labels "breakfast," "lunch," and "dinner." Then, children and adults of Arab culture were asked to do the same. The results confirmed the hypothesis that time perception is influenced by education and culture. "Whereas English speakers placed breakfast on the left and dinner on the right of lunch, Arabic speakers preferred the opposite arrangement, consistent with the direction of reading and writing in English and Arabic, and with the lateral organization of time on calendars in English- and Arabic-speaking cultures" (Casasanto & Jasmin, 2012, p. 648).

The lateral axis of time also influences the logic of planning when managers are structuring their charts and tables with events, responsibilities, and deadlines. A simple example is the Gantt chart, which contains time sequences for achieving proposed objectives. These sequences are arranged along the lateral left–right axis. "The proposed strategy then results in the habit of placing earlier events on the left mental space followed by later events being located more to the right" (Ouellet et al., 2010, p. 312).

The conclusion is that *time* is a complex entity, and we should consider both its subjective and objective dimensions. Although the *physical time* measured by the clock and learned through education is dominant in managerial logic and decision-making, *psychological time* cannot be ignored since it influences our perception of events, duration and correlation, and strategy design.

We see and understand the world where we live through *thinking models* (Fauconnier & Turner, 2002; Senge, 1999). A thinking model is a conceptual system, developed through education and individual effort, which presents a simplifying image of the world based on cognitive and emotional approximations. The real world is infinite in any dimension or depth, so the only way to understand it and make sense of it is to create approximations of its complexity. The more developed our thinking model, the better these approximations are. Research in psychology and cognitive science leads to the conclusion that our thinking model results from the interaction of two systems of thinking that coexist in our minds. "*System 1* operates automatically and quickly, with little or no effort and no sense of voluntary control" (Kahneman, 2011, p. 20). System 1 is based on the reactions of our sensory system to external stimuli. It generates emotions and feelings and creates complex neural maps and patterns of ideas. "*System 2* allocates attention to the effortful mental activities that demand it, including complex computations" (Kahneman, 2011, p. 21). This is our rational system of thinking, which transforms neural maps and patterns of ideas into thoughts and theories.

It is interesting to see now how our thinking models incorporate *time* as an independent variable. From this perspective, we may distinguish three main thinking models: inertial thinking, dynamic thinking, and entropic thinking (Bolisani & Bratianu, 2018). *Inertial thinking* can be understood by analogy with inertial forces in physics, which resist change. The inertial thinking model does not contain time as a variable. It is the simplest thinking model with respect to time, and it generates a state of psychological stability and safety because things around us remain unchanged and events can be easily anticipated. Inertial thinking creates routines and functional automatisms, which allow us to perform simple actions almost without thinking, like locking and unlocking the door of the house or preparing coffee in the morning. Inertial thinking opposes change by transforming itself into a resistance force. Inertial thinking is powerful in organizational change because people who cannot see the reason for a change will oppose it, seeking to keep things as they are (Doz & Kosonen, 2008; Kotter, 2008). For inertial thinking, there is no future, only a continuous present. The future appears as an extension or extrapolation of the present with no significant change, as in uniform motion. As Rumelt (2012, p. 203) observes, "An organization's greatest challenge may not be external threats or opportunities, but the effects of entropy and inertia."

The *dynamic thinking model* incorporates time, but only through its quantitative dimension. It is like physics, where processes are considered *reversible* and thus the direction of motion is meaningless. In the well-known formula for computing the average velocity (V) of any vehicle, $V = D/T$, D stands for distance and T for time. But this reference to time represents only units of time (i.e., seconds, minutes, hours), and it is valid for any direction of motion. Dynamic thinking is better than inertial thinking because it can represent motion and change, but it is a construct only for reversible processes. A process is *reversible* if it can return to its initial conditions, passing through the same equilibrium states. It looks like time is flying in circles, as it is in Taoism: "Returning – moving in endless cycles – is the basic pattern of movement of the Tao" (Nisbett, 2003, p. 14). It is an ideal process used in theory to simplify the complexity of the real world. Because of that simplification, the past, the present, and the future are interchangeable components of the time structure. Real processes are *irreversible*, and the past, the present, and the future are aligned along a unidirectional axis.

The *entropic thinking model* incorporates time with both its qualitative and quantitative dimensions. Organizational and social processes are irreversible, and they need a full-time framework that contains a complete structure composed of *past, present,* and *future*. Time is flying from the *past* toward the *present* and from the *present* toward the *future* in a continuous, uniform, and irreversible way. Since the irreversibility of thermodynamic processes could have been explained by using the concept of *entropy*, we may call this thinking pattern *entropic*. The concept of *entropy* was introduced by Rudolf Clausius in 1865 to explain the transfer of heat from a body with a high temperature to a body with a low temperature, and the relationship between heat transfer and mechanical work. This is known as the second law of thermodynamics. Ludwig Boltzmann developed a computational formula for *absolute entropy*, which became famous in statistical mechanics (Atkins, 2010; Georgescu-Roegen, 1999). Because of its semantic power, *entropy* has been used in many other science domains by semantic extension (Bratianu, 2019; Chaldize, 2000; Zhou et al., 2013).

Entropic thinking is a characteristic of visionary leaders. They can define the objectives to be accomplished and then design strategies to achieve those objectives under the pressure of uncertainty and absence of knowledge (De Geus, 2002; Gerstner, 2003; Isaacson, 2011).

2.2 The Probable Future

Newtonian logic based on linearity and deterministic thinking (Stacey et al., 2000), coupled with the mechanistic modeling of organizations based on the machine metaphor (Morgan, 1997), leads to the idea that the future is an extension of the present, which means that it is predictable.

Deterministic thinking is based on the assumption that things around us and the events we encounter in our daily life are well defined and well known. Their behavior can be anticipated from the knowledge we have. As Knight (2006, p. 204) remarks, "We have, then, our dogma which is the presupposition of knowledge, in this form; that the world is made up of *things*, which, *under the same circumstances*, always *behave in the same way*." They are certain. Think about the law of energy conservation or the law of entropy. For the same initial and boundary conditions, the processes will always unfold in the same way. They are fully predictable. People strive for certainty because it generates a psychological state of comfort and safety (Kahneman, 2011). Deterministic thinking is necessary for science and engineering since technology must perform in fully controlled ways.

Having a mechanical engineering education, Frederick Winslow Taylor introduced deterministic thinking as the dominant logic in scientific management (Taylor, 1998). Later on, Max Weber developed a theory about bureaucracy in public administration based on deterministic thinking and the machine metaphor. He conceived of bureaucracy "as a form of organization that emphasizes precision, speed, clarity, regularity, reliability, and efficiency achieved through the creation of a fixed division of tasks, hierarchical supervision, and detailed rules and regulations" (Morgan, 1997, p. 17). *Command-and-control* management is also a result of deterministic thinking, based on planning for a predictable and controllable future. The same idea led to strategic planning as a linear extrapolation of the present state and some identifiable trends (Mintzberg, 2000).

In a turbulent business environment with fast and unpredictable changes, deterministic thinking cannot provide reliable solutions for the future. The absence of knowledge and the randomness of events generate a state of *uncertainty*. Deterministic thinking cannot deal with uncertainty, and it must be replaced with *probabilistic thinking*. Knight explains this change in our thinking mode:

> The fundamental fact underlying probability reasoning is generally assumed to be our ignorance. *If* it were possible to measure with absolute accuracy all the determining circumstances in the case, it would seem that we should be able to predict the result in the individual instance, but it is obtrusively manifest that in many cases, we cannot do this. (Knight, 2006, p. 218)

When considering probabilities, we should be aware of the difference between *objective* probabilities and *subjective* probabilities (Kahneman, 2011; Knight, 2006; Lindley, 2006). While objective probabilities can be computed based on statistical data, the subjective ones express our beliefs about uncertain events in the real world. The two types of probability are linked through our cognitive relationship with the external world, as underlined by Lindley (2006, p. 38): "probability expresses a relationship between a person, you, and the real world. It is not solely a feature of your mind; it is not a value possessed by an event but expresses a relationship between you and the event and is a basic tool in your understanding of the world."

Understanding the past means interpreting data we have about past events and their consequences. Understanding the future means using our imagination to compensate for the absence of knowledge and to reduce uncertainty about some events and phenomena. Since *risks* are always associated with uncertainty, *risk analysis* is very useful in evaluating the possible effects of our decisions on the development of our enterprise and providing rational support for risk management. The aim of risk management is to maximize the area where some control over the outcomes can be established and to minimize opposite situations (Bernstein, 1998). Discussing uncertainty, Spender (2014) remarks that beyond *ignorance* generated by the absence of knowledge, there is *incommensurability*, which reflects the absence of an adequate metric to measure the knowledge gap, and *indeterminacy*, which reflects the unknown ways people might act in some future contexts. "Thus, in addition to 'ignorance' and 'incommensurability,' people generate 'indeterminacy' as they respond actively to each other and change in ways contingent on that action. The firm's context becomes interactive, dynamic in a different way" (Spender, 2014, p. 11). The aim of the firm in such an uncertain environment is to expand and exploit the "opportunity space" (Spender & Strong, 2014, p. 10).

The difficulty in understanding the future comes primarily from the fact that the human mind is averse to dealing with uncertainty and risk (Kahneman, 2011; Taleb, 2007). Decision-making is influenced by the probable gains and losses that come from the option chosen. Many experiments have shown that people are more sensitive to probable losses than gains from their choices. Kahneman and Tversky developed the *prospect theory* for dealing with psychological aspects of decision-making under the pressure of uncertainty. They showed that previous economic theories based solely on financial values could not predict the way people make their decisions for future actions. They revealed the importance of emotions in dealing with risks and probable losses (Kahneman, 2011).

In the paradigm of *deterministic thinking*, researchers discuss only one future, which is ahead of the present time. We go toward that future, as suggested by the moving observer metaphor. In the paradigm of *probabilistic thinking*, we may have several plausible futures, several probable scenarios (van der Heijden et al., 2002; MacKay & McKiernan, 2018). Although our existence is confined to only one present, and it will continue in only one future, we may imagine several probable futures as alternatives to present trends and expectations. The basic philosophy is not to predict the future but to create alternatives for a possible future by using *foresight* and *scenario thinking* (De Ruijter & Alkema, 2014; Murgatroyd, 2015; van der Laan & Yap, 2016). Even if none of the designed scenarios happen, the future will contain many of their characteristics. Also, by designing many probable futures, we can learn how to reduce uncertainty and the absence of knowledge – how to "create" knowledge and move faster from the state of *known-knowns* toward *unknown-unknowns* (Bolisani & Bratianu, 2018; Dalkir, 2005).

The future can also be seen as *chaos* resulting from turbulence in the business environment and from the tensions between order and disorder, continuity and discontinuity (Gleick, 2008; Stacey et al., 2000). This interpretation of the future as chaos clashes with the deterministic extrapolation of the future, and it challenges our imagination. The disruptive innovations which cannot be anticipated can be associated with that chaotic future, although each of them extracts some knowledge from the past and the present (Isaacson, 2014). One may consider the probable future has a higher likelihood of unfolding in front of us as a *strange attractor*, with a knowledge pattern that can be understood. "A strange attractor displays a recognizable pattern in space or over time, but that pattern is irregular. In other words, strange attractors are paradoxically regular and irregular, stable and unstable, at the same time" (Stacey et al., 2000, p. 87). By considering an organization as a dynamic system and its strategy as a driving force for achieving a competitive advantage in a probable future, that future might be interpreted as a strange attractor.

3 Knowledge As a Strategic Resource

3.1 The Resource-Based View of the Firm

The Resource-Based View (RBV) of the firm (Barney, 1991; Barney & Hesterly, 2012) was developed to complement the competitive strategic analysis of a firm initiated by Porter (1980, 1985). While Porter looks outside the firm to understand the competition in the market and to identify the dominant forces shaping that competition, Barney is looking inside the firm, searching for the most relevant resources and capabilities for achieving competitive advantage. "The resource-based view perceives the firm as a unique bundle of idiosyncratic resources and capabilities where the primary task of management is to maximize value through the optimal deployment of existing resources and capabilities while developing the firm's resource base for the future" (Grant, 1996, p. 110). Thus, the quality and quantity of a firm's resources become a necessary condition for the firm to create a sustainable competitive advantage. According to Barney and Hesterly (2012), the core resources should be valuable, unique or rare, and costly to imitate.

An insightful analysis of a firm's resources and of their role in the growth of the firm was performed by Penrose (1959). She makes a clear distinction between tangible and intangible resources. *Tangible* resources can be seen, can be touched, and, as a consequence, can be measured. Tangible resources are buildings, land, technological equipment, raw materials, and all physical objects used in the production process. *Intangible* resources cannot be seen or touched, and thus their measurement is a real challenge for managers. Intangible resources are the knowledge and experience of employees, patents, brands, the firm's image, and organizational and cultural values. Human resources represent an integration of these types since our bodies are tangible but our knowledge is intangible. Penrose introduces the idea that *resources* should be considered together with the *services* they render: "Strictly speaking, it is never *resources* themselves that are the 'inputs' in the production process, but only the *services* that the resources can render" (Penrose, 2013, p. 25). The main distinction between resources and their associated services is the correlation with their use. Both resources and their associated services can be expanded by increasing the knowledge necessary to use them more efficiently. That knowledge can be obtained from the internal business environment through research and innovation and from the external business environment through acquisition: "we should not ignore the effect of increased experience and knowledge of the external world and the effect of changes in the external world" (Penrose, 2013, p. 79).

Building on Polanyi's (1983) demonstration of the *tacit dimension* of knowledge and on the iceberg metaphor, Nonaka and Takeuchi (1995) developed the theory of the knowledge dyad composed of explicit and tacit knowledge. *Explicit* knowledge is the rational and objective knowledge that can be expressed by using a natural or a symbolic language. It is the *know-that* (Ryle, 2002) or *know-what* (Davenport & Prusak, 2000) knowledge about the external world. Explicit knowledge is acquired through education and can be easily transferred through social interactions. It is illustrated by the visible part of an iceberg. *Tacit* knowledge is subjective and hard to express by using body language and transferring it to a social context. It is represented by the hidden part of the iceberg, which is underwater.

> Tacit knowledge is personal and hard to formalize, making it difficult to communicate or to share with others. Subjective insights, intuitions, and hunches fall into this category of knowledge. Furthermore, tacit knowledge is deeply rooted in an individual's action and experience, as well as in the ideals, values, or emotions he or she embraces. (Nonaka & Takeuchi, 1995, p. 8)

Tacit knowledge is a direct result of experiential learning (Kolb, 2015), and it is the *know-how* knowledge (Davenport & Prusak, 2000; Rhem, 2017). It can be transformed into explicit knowledge through the *externalization* process in the Socialization, Externalization, Combination, and Internalization (SECI) model suggested by Nonaka (1994) and developed further by Nonaka and Takeuchi (1995), Nonaka and Toyama (2003), and Nonaka et al. (2008). Explicit knowledge can be transformed into tacit knowledge through the process of *internalization* in the same SECI model. Explicit knowledge is a product of the conscious brain, while tacit knowledge is processed by the unconscious cognitive brain (Damasio, 2003, 2012; Frith, 2007).

Because tacit knowledge is deeply rooted in individual experience and its transferability is limited, it cannot be imitated easily. That makes tacit knowledge unique, and it contributes significantly to competitive advantage. Extending that observation to organizational knowledge, Spender (1996, p. 46) remarks: "Since the origin of all tangible resources lies outside the firm, it follows that competitive advantage is more likely to arise from the intangible firm-specific knowledge which enables it to add value to the incoming factors of production in a relatively unique manner."

Explicit knowledge can be easily codified and embedded in the firm's databases, routines, and technological procedures. Knowledge codification is a condition for knowledge sharing and knowledge exploitation (Balconi, 2002; Bratianu, 2015a; Rhem, 2017). Knowledge codification increases the efficiency of knowledge processing significantly, and it supports organizational learning (Argote, 2013; Argote & Miron-Spektor, 2011; Senge, 1999). Knowledge codification can be enhanced by information technology and organizational culture.

Going beyond the metaphors of knowledge as *flows* (Nissen, 2006) and *stocks-and-flows* (Bolisani & Oltramari, 2012; Nonaka et al., 2008), Bratianu (2011) introduced the metaphor of knowledge as *energy* and developed the theory of *knowledge fields* (Bratianu, 2015a; Bratianu & Bejinaru, 2019). According to this theory, knowledge is manifested in three fundamental fields: rational knowledge, emotional knowledge, and spiritual knowledge. This is in concordance with Spender's remark, "as a practicing manager dealing with real colleagues, I believe we need a theory that pays more explicit attention to the emotional, moral, and social dimensions of organizational activity" (Spender, 2003, p. 267).

Rational knowledge is expressed as explicit knowledge and represents the objective component of the complex knowledge field. It is the result of our reflection on the information received by the brain from the sensory system. Rational knowledge is the final result of the learning process, and it is the backbone of the whole educational system. *Emotional knowledge* is a component of tacit knowledge and is created by our emotions and feelings (Damasio, 2012; Frith, 2007; LeDoux, 1999; Nussbaum, 2001). Emotional knowledge is a kind of wordless knowledge: "The simplest form in which the wordless knowledge emerges mentally is the feeling of knowing – the feeling of what happens when an organism is engaged with the processing of an object – and that only thereafter can inferences and interpretations begin to occur regarding the feeling of knowing" (Damasio, 1999, p. 26). Emotional knowledge plays an important role in decision-making, especially when managers are under time pressure and in conditions of uncertainty. Intuition is based mainly on emotional knowledge (Hill, 2008; Klein, 2003; Simon, 1987). *Spiritual knowledge* represents the set of values and meanings concerning our existence. In a firm, spiritual knowledge is a part of the organizational culture. As Maxwell (2007, p. 274) suggests, "We have to learn to see aspects of the world around us: stones, people, trees, sky. Equally, we have to learn to see meaning and value in the world around us, in our environment, in events, in human actions and lives." Only by setting our aspirations high can we reach the top level of self-actualization on Maslow's hierarchy of needs and achieve the degree of satisfaction we need in life.

The theory of knowledge fields also introduces a new type of knowledge dynamics. While the model developed by Nonaka (1994) and his collaborators (Nonaka & Takeuchi, 1995; Nonaka et al., 2008) is focused only on the transformation between explicit and tacit knowledge, and the Nissen (2006) model is based on the fluid mechanics analogy, the knowledge dynamics model developed by Bratianu (2015a) reflects the transformations between different fields of knowledge, at any time and in any social context. This knowledge dynamics model contributes substantially to the decision-making process (Bratianu & Vatamanescu, 2018) and to understanding the dynamic capabilities (Teece, 2009) of the firm.

A *capability* represents the managerial capacity of a team or organization to use its resources efficiently. The RBV of the firm integrates both resources and capabilities in designing strategies for achieving a competitive advantage. In this perspective, knowledge becomes a *strategic resource* and the raw material for constructing knowledge dynamic capabilities. It is *strategic* because its contribution is conceived in a long-term framework and its specificity cannot be imitated by competitors. Also, knowledge is the basic ingredient of the firm's intellectual capital (Andriessen, 2004; Ricceri, 2008; Sveiby, 2001) and the most fundamental resource for dealing with uncertainty and designing deliberate strategies in knowledge management (Grant, 1997; Ichijo, 2007; Roth, 1996; Rother, 2010).

One strategic capability a firm may develop is organizational learning (Argote, 2013; Argyris, 1999; Örtenblad, 2011; Wellman, 2009). This is a complex process developed at the team or organizational level which integrates individual learning and creates synergy in learning outcomes. Organizational learning does not happen automatically. The alternative could be the Albrecht phenomenon (2003, p. 4): "Intelligent people, when assembled into an organization, will tend toward collective stupidity." This phenomenon should be avoided by adopting a strategic approach for developing organizational learning, and then extending that process throughout the firm and creating the necessary conditions for transforming the firm into a learning organization (Argote, 2013; Senge, 1999). According to Senge (1999, p. 13), "A learning organization is a place where people are continually discovering how they create their reality. And how they can change it." A learning organization is capable of achieving a sustainable competitive advantage, which is the most important objective in a firm's strategic framework, and succeeding in a turbulent business environment because of its capacity to deal with uncertainty and absence of knowledge.

3.2 The Knowledge-Based Theory of the Firm

Any theory of the firm represents a *conceptual model* of real firms and the role they play in economics and society. That model is based on a well-defined set of hypotheses and principles, and it has an explanatory or behavioral role. From an economic perspective, the theory of the firm focuses on the ownership and control of resources and their transformation into products and services in ways that lead to maximizing the shareholders' profit. For Coase (1937, p. 393), a firm "consists of the system of relationships which comes into existence when the direction of resources is dependent on an entrepreneur." For Penrose (2013, p. 24), a firm "is more than an administrative unit; it is also a collection of productive resources the disposal of which between different uses and over time is determined by administrative decisions." In her analysis, Penrose is searching for those economic factors that influence the growth of the firm in a given macroeconomic environment.

Switching from the economic perspective toward a sociological one, Simon (1991, p. 39) considers that "organizations are best viewed as systems of interrelated roles, and that is the way I have been viewing them here." Thus, Simons focuses on people as decision-makers and goal-oriented agents. He comes to support Penrose's idea that a firm is more than a bundle of resources and that analyzing them based only on the pricing mechanism is too limited to yield valuable solutions for predicting the firm's behavior. Adopting a constructivist approach, Spender (2015) considers firms as social institutions constructed with the purpose of finding solutions to the problems causing social anxiety. They are "opportunity spaces" for reducing uncertainty by eliminating the absence of knowledge (Spender & Strong, 2014, p. 10).

The *knowledge-based theory of the firm* is an alternative to the economic formulation. It opens a new perspective on the complexity of the firm, especially of the knowledge-intensive firm (Bolisani et al., 2013; Doloreaux et al., 2010; Landry et al., 2012). "A knowledge-based theory of the firm can yield insights beyond the production-function and resource-based theories of the firm. It is a platform for a new view of the firm as a dynamic, evolving, quasi-autonomous system of knowledge production and application" (Spender, 1996, p. 59).

Any firm can be conceived as *a system of systems* (Jackson, 2019), and each system has a certain structure and a process. In the knowledge-based theory of the firm, the components of the system are represented by their knowledge content, and the structure is supported by the managerial hierarchy and the distribution of information technology. The process results from the integration of all microprocesses of knowledge creation, acquisition, sharing, codification, transfer, transformation, and application. According to Brown and Duguid (1998, p. 90), "All firms are in essence knowledge organizations. Their ability to outperform the marketplace rests on the continuous generation and synthesis of collective, organizational knowledge." The same conclusion comes from Nickerson and Zenger (2004). Tsoukas (1996) considers that a firm is essentially a distributed knowledge system, and organizational knowledge is a result of the integration of individual knowledge, in both explicit and tacit forms. Since knowledge resources have a nonlinear behavior (Bratianu, 2009), all organizational processes are based on *integration* and not on *summation*. Unfortunately, many researchers cannot make the distinction between linearity and nonlinearity, so they use linear operations like in accounting to define and evaluate knowledge and intellectual capital (Bratianu, 2018a; Dumay, 2016). According to Grant (1996, p. 117), a firm can be conceived as a "knowledge-integrating institution."

A key feature of a knowledge system is the fact that it is open to knowledge fluxes crossing its interface with the external environment, which is conceived as a knowledge environment. The knowledge dynamics of the firm conceived as a knowledge system comprise the following distinct processes: knowledge creation, knowledge acquisition, knowledge sharing, knowledge transfer, knowledge transformation, knowledge loss, and knowledge retention. The purpose of knowledge management is to create a dynamic equilibrium between all of these processes and a sustainable equilibrium at the interface with knowledge systems from the external environment (Bratianu, 2015a; Kodama, 2011). Without the continuous effort of managers to integrate knowledge processes, there will be a tendency to increase the knowledge entropy of the firm and, as a consequence, to increase its knowledge risks (Bratianu, 2019; Durst, 2019; Durst & Zieba, 2017).

The knowledge-based theory of the firm is a conceptual model of real firms that incorporates the knowledge of individual employees in the emergent organizational knowledge. The main hypotheses in the design of the knowledge model are:

- The theory focuses on the knowledge system, which is in continuous inter-action with all the other systems defined for the whole system of the firm.
- The knowledge system is an open system, having porous boundaries with the external knowledge environment.
- The knowledge system is dynamic and nonlinear.
- The knowledge system contains knowledge resources, knowledge capabilities, and the decision-making processes concerning these entities.
- The evolution of the knowledge system is conceived within a strategic framework.

It is important to understand that the knowledge system is open, and thus its interface with the external environment can be crossed in both directions by knowledge flows or fluxes. We talk about *knowledge flows* when using the stocks-and-flows metaphor and about *knowledge fluxes* when using the energy metaphor. Both expressions reflect the same reality, but with different degrees of accuracy. Knowledge flows when there is a difference in the knowing pressure between the endpoints of the flow. Knowledge fluxes are generated by the nonuniformity of the knowledge fields, and an imbalance of knowledge between two locations. Many researchers do not understand that natural condition, and they ignore it in discussions of knowledge sharing and knowledge transfer.

Although the literature about the nonlinearity of the knowledge field is very scarce, we have to understand that this property is critical in designing metrics for knowledge evaluation. All the metrics imagined so far for measuring intellectual capital as a potential of intangibles are based on linear metrics. This demonstrates how difficult it is to escape linear thinking and practice. The same is true for understanding the evolution of different processes and phenomena with nonlinear correlations between inputs and outputs. In such a case, there is no proportionality between causes and final effects, which creates real difficulties in anticipating the evolution of the knowledge system and in using economic indicators based on linear metrics like *efficiency* and *productivity*. Drucker (2001) offers an insightful comparison of the manual worker's productivity and the knowledge worker's productivity. He notes that in the first case we consider the *quantity* of the work performed in a given period, while in the second case we should consider the *quality* of the work. "Quality is the essence of the output. In judging the performance of a teacher, we do not ask how many students there can be in his or her class. We ask how many students learn anything – and that's a quality question" (Drucker, 2001, p. 143). However, measuring the quality of knowledge is much more difficult than measuring its quantity, even if a metric to measure the quantity of knowledge has not been created. Stam (2007) considers that in any knowledge system, knowledge as an intangible resource represents potential, and the system transforms that potential into action, ending up with products and services. This approach is in line with the theory of nonlinear integrators (Bratianu, 2013). In that perspective, the notion of productivity gets a new meaning: "If one accepts as true that knowledge has become our main source of relative advantage and intellectual capital is new wealth, then the process of transforming this resource into wealth has become the new challenge. Within this research, the process of transforming knowledge into a value is referred to as *knowledge productivity*" (Stam, 2007, p. 5).

Any system has at least one specific law that conditions the behavior of the system components or their interconnection. For instance, if we consider a building as a mechanical system, then the specific law that conditions the behavior of the components is the law of gravity. In a knowledge system, we consider that the *law of entropy* acts as a specific law (Bratianu & Bejinaru, 2019). However, it is an extension of the second law of thermodynamics (Atkins, 2010; Georgescu-Roegen, 1999). *Entropy* is a concept introduced in thermodynamics in 1865 by Rudolf Clausius as a measure of the behavior of thermal systems – namely, of the change in their state as a result of the transfer of heat or of the transformation of heat into mechanical work. The concept evolved into a computational formula derived by Ludwig Boltzmann, which shows the correlation between the probability distribution of a set of microstates and the emerging macrostate of a thermal system. Claude Shannon (1948), in a seminal paper about the mathematical theory of communication, introduces the concept of *information* and a computational formula for *information entropy*, which is similar to that of Boltzmann. Changing the inquiring domain to that of knowledge management, Bratianu (2019) explores the possibility of extending the concept of *entropy* to the theory of knowledge fields and measuring the knowledge distribution in a certain firm.

In the theory of knowledge fields (Bratianu & Bejinaru, 2019), one form of knowledge can be transformed into any other form of knowledge, generating continuous knowledge dynamics governed by the law of entropy. For instance, emotional knowledge can be transformed into rational knowledge, and vice versa, as a result of cooperation between the two systems of thinking described by Kahneman (2011). These knowledge dynamics should be stimulated by transformational leaders through organizational change. Kotter (2008) suggests that the old paradigm of *analyzing–thinking–changing* be replaced with a new one based on the transformation *seeing–feeling–changing*, which incorporates knowledge dynamics.

The last hypothesis reflects the need to consider any knowledge system within a strategic framework, since knowledge is a strategic resource for the firm and it can contribute to achieving a sustainable competitive advantage only from a long-term perspective. Knowledge is a product of a learning process, regardless of the particular way of doing it, and learning is a time-dependent process. Furthermore, developing the capability of *learning to learn* needs time, especially when it is scaled up to the level of the whole firm, transforming it into a learning organization (Argote, 2013; Örtenblad, 2011; Senge, 1999). A learning organization develops double-loop learning (Argyris, 1999) and the capacity for producing generative knowledge (Senge, 1999). If *adaptive* knowledge can be a solution for a short time, *generative* knowledge is necessary for achieving a sustainable competitive advantage. Thus, the learning organization can be understood only through the lens of the knowledge system emerging within a certain firm, in a given business environment, and with given initial and boundary conditions. Initial conditions position the evolution of the firm with respect to a time frame, while boundary conditions contribute to understanding the knowledge transfer between firms and how to minimize knowledge risks by controlling the knowledge fluxes across the firm's boundary. As firms grow, their boundary changes, and that influences the behavior of the knowledge system and the strategizing process to reduce uncertainty and the absence of knowledge.

4 Strategy Design and Strategizing

4.1 From Planning to Strategizing

Management is a process that needs time to be realized. As Drucker (1993, p. 44) explains, "The time dimension is inherent in management because management is concerned with decisions for action. And action always aims at results in the future." Thus, management integrates the *present* and the *future* into a continuum with a linear variation. Although Drucker (1993) considers the future as a discontinuity from the present time, in management, the future is just an extension of the present. Initially, when Frederick Winslow Taylor developed scientific management, the future extension was only for one or several days. Planning was a result of the asymmetric distribution of knowledge between the managers and the workers. Managers had the knowledge of defining the worker's tasks and how these tasks were to be done. "The work of every workman is fully planned out by the management at least one day in advance, and each man receives in most cases complete written instructions, describing in detail the task which he is to accomplish, as well as the means to be used in doing the work" (Taylor, 1998, p. 17).

From individual tasks and the immediate future represented by a couple of days, *planning* developed to the higher levels of organizations and longer futures for up to one year. Any complex activity is broken down into its components, and each component is analyzed with respect to the time needed for its realization. Then the components are projected on a time domain and ordered in a logical sequence for their completion. The time chart used for such a representation is called a *Gantt chart* after the name of its inventor. It is interesting to note that Henry Gantt developed that time chart about the time Frederick Winslow Taylor was developing his theory of scientific management, at the beginning of the last century. In the basic structure of a Gantt chart, all the tasks to be performed for a certain project are placed on the vertical axis, and the time intervals or durations of these tasks are placed on the horizontal axis.

Planning is based on deterministic and linear thinking models. By using a deterministic thinking model, planning eliminates uncertainty and considers a static external business environment. The linear thinking model appears as a result of using the time metric, which is linear. With the emergence of project management, where experts use advanced probabilistic computational models and risk analysis methods, planning lost some of its rigidity and became more flexible. The logic of planning now incorporates change both inside and outside of an organization, and it aims at reducing uncertainty and improving managerial decisions (Robbins & DeCenzo, 2005). Also, planning reduces overlapping activities by structuring them into a unidirectional flow toward the future. The result of planning is a working framework that is used to facilitate managerial control. One of the most important features of planning is its formalization (Mintzberg, 2000). Any formalization introduces inflexibility into an organization, which manifests as resistance to a change process.

When the external business environment became more dynamic, and the competition in the market increased significantly, top managers acknowledged the need for long-range planning that transformed over time into *strategic planning* (Drucker, 1993; Mintzberg, 2000; Mintzberg et al., 1998; Nonaka & Zhu, 2012). Strategic planning continued to use the rational approach for problem formulation and solution search, in accordance with the general attitude of the "scientification of business strategy," as remarked by Nonaka and Zhu (2012). However, in many situations, the conventional thinking model proved to be harmful (Haig, 2003; Mintzberg, 2000; Rumelt, 2012). Thus, the dominance of rationality and analytical techniques generated limitations in understanding the future and in searching for long-term solutions to economic and managerial problems. One of these limitations was to consider the future as an extension of the present and not as a new time structure with increasing uncertainty and absence of knowledge compared with the present, where determining factors are mostly well defined. For instance, focusing on achieving high efficiency at each moment of time in our march toward the future does not guarantee an overall efficient solution. That is because local and momentary optimized solutions do not necessarily aggregate into a global or long-term efficient solution. The good solutions for today might not be good for future problems because of changes in the context and time dynamics of the many variables in those possible problems. Strategic planning is based on the moving observer and stationary time metaphor. That means we march toward a known future and plan for a final solution that is composed of a series of successive approximations. The logic is good for a predictable environment, but today's data show a very dynamic and unpredictable business environment with many turbulent components and hardly anticipated economic crises. For such a reality, strategic planning based on deterministic thinking cannot be a reliable managerial tool anymore. Deterministic thinking leads to *deterministic planning* (Mintzberg, 2000). However, the approach of a deterministic framework turned out to be a fallacy of strategic planning because the evolution of the environment cannot be predetermined. The collapse of the centrally planned economies in the former socialist European countries demonstrated clearly the limitations of linear and deterministic planning when applied in a turbulent economic environment.

It is clear that a thinking model based on determinism and linearity cannot support strategic conceptual work. The future conceived as an extension of the present time, unfolding progressively like an algorithm, should be changed into a complex time structure with multiple possible configurations and distributions of probabilities. It is a possible future model characterized primarily by uncertainty and the absence of knowledge. Understanding such a future and thinking about how to analyze new problems and search for adequate solutions represents a different mental approach. Spender (2014) calls this *strategic work*. Strategists should integrate *imagination* and *rationality* in their approaches to the future and look for solutions to reduce the degree of uncertainty and the anxiety it generates. In a synthetic formulation, Spender (2014, p. xvi) concludes that "Strategizing is the process of dealing with anxiety." For managers, strategizing should be a continuous process since anxiety about the future cannot be eliminated from real life. It is like the horizon paradox: whenever we go to meet the horizon, the horizon moves with us such that we can never catch up with it. Fortunately, we don't want to control the whole future, but only that part of it where we project the firm's objectives. We may call that specific part the *desirable* or *preferable* future. It is that future in which we identify the firm's opportunity space and for which we design the business model and define the firm's objectives.

Nonaka and Takeuchi (1995) stress the importance of tacit knowledge, insight, and intuition for the strategic work of Japanese managers, which is the essential difference between them and American managers, whose thinking is mostly based on rationality. Japanese strategists learn how to make efficient use of their cognitive unconscious. As Ohmae (1982, p. 4) remarked, "In what I call the mind of the strategist, insight and a consequent drive for achievement, often amounting to a sense of mission, fuel a thought process which is basically creative and intuitive rather rational." Rational analysis is not ignored, but it comes after the intuitive stage and transforms thought into a fully conscious process (Kahneman, 2011; Lakoff & Johnson, 1999; Ohmae, 1982).

The legendary martial artist Miyamoto Musashi, in his famous *Book of Five Rings*, focused on the essential role of strategizing in a warrior's training for winning battles. Searching for knowledge should start with knowledge from inside the individual and his experience, and only then look for knowledge in the external world. Among Musashi's basic principles of strategizing, the following fit very well with the strategic thinking model discussed above: a) strive for inner judgment and an understanding of everything; b) see that which cannot be seen; c) overlook nothing, regardless of its insignificance (Kaufman, 1994, p. 21). As Spender (2014) emphasized, that inner judgment should integrate imagination and rationality to reach a holistic understanding of the complexity and dynamics of the problem to be solved. To see that which cannot be seen looks almost impossible, but it is a competence the strategist should develop to discover some trends in the external business environment and to anticipate possible events, especially those which seem to be very improbable. These "black swan" events (Taleb, 2007) may have decisive consequences for the firm's business. To see into the future, leaders should develop their *vision* as a framework for strategizing. "Because the way forward lies in the future and because no one can see into the future, leaders are trying to foresee the unforeseeable. This requires imagination and the ability to create a vision of the future" (Wootton & Horne, 2010, p. 6).

4.2 From Strategizing to Strategy Design

4.2.1 The Strategy Design Ontology

In his *theory of opportunism*, Barnard (1938) discusses managerial decisions made under conditions of uncertainty generated by the future, and how rational analysis combines with intuition. The decision should be context-dependent, where the context is conceived in its dynamic evolution. All the factors influencing decision-making should be divided into two categories: a) critical factors and b) all the others. For Barnard, critical factors were those that decisively influence the course of action. He called them "limiting" if they reflect some tangible physical elements, or "strategic" if they reflect intangible elements like knowledge or organizational factors. "The limiting (strategic) factor is the one whose control, in the right form, at the right place, and time will establish a new system or set of conditions which meets the purpose" (Barnard, 1968, p. 203). These strategic factors have an objective existence and are context-dependent. However, identifying them as critical is based on the subjective experience and intuition of the organizational leaders (Nussbaum, 2001; Rumelt, 2012).

If *strategizing* is the process of thinking for the future and "managing uncertainty, opportunity, and enterprise" in the vision of Spender (2014), then *the strategy* is the integrated result of that process (Nonaka & Zhu, 2012; Mintzberg et al., 1998; Whittington, 2001). There are many interpretations and definitions of strategy, but we are not looking for the best definition or a unique semantic structure. We consider that a strategy is the result of a complex process of decision-making, dependent on the dynamics of a competitive context, and oriented toward an important objective. Having a dynamic semantic, a strategy can be understood only within a well-defined framework and integrated into a given school of thought. We have to accept multiple semantic models and a large spectrum of pragmatic implementations. Our presentation is based on the excellent syntheses by Whittington (2001) and Mintzberg et al. (1998) of strategies and their schools of thought.

Whittington (2001) conceives a framework for analyzing strategy models and theories based on a matrix. The horizontal dimension is for the criteria for defining the goal of the strategy. Thus, it is a single-criterion situation when focusing on profit-maximization, and a multiple-criteria situation when decision-makers consider both economic and non-economic criteria for achieving sustainability. The vertical dimension reflects the two time–space metaphors presented in Section 2. The metaphor of the moving observer considers time stationary and the future as an extension of the present time. That allows managers to design deliberate strategies. The metaphor of moving time considers the observer stationary and the future as a series of events coming toward him. In such a case, managers should be prepared to design emergent strategies. An illustration of the ontology matrix is presented in Figure 1.

The classical strategy approach. The classical approach to strategy is based on the hypotheses of dealing with a stationary or quasi-stationary external business environment and using the profit-maximization theory as the only criterion for achieving a long-term economic advantage. Although the profit-maximization managerial practice aims at short-term results, the effort to extend the present time into the future led to the assumption of a linear extrapolation of profitability. Classical strategy design is incorporated in almost all textbooks because it is in line with these economic principles. The founders of the deliberate strategies

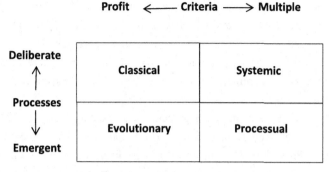

Figure 1 Perspectives on strategy

were Chandler (1962), Ansoff (1965), and Sloan (1963). They defined the main features of designing deliberate strategies: the rational analysis of the internal and external business environments, aiming at profit-maximization, and separating the design phase from the implementation phase. Alfred Sloan, a former president of General Motors, emphasized the paramount importance of profit-maximization and how managers should select those markets where their firms could obtain the highest profits. In Sloan's (1963, p. 49) view, "the strategic aim of a business is to earn a return on capital, and if in any particular case the return, in the long run, is not satisfactory, the deficiency should be corrected or the activity should be abandoned."

As a visionary leader in the era of industrial management, Alfred Sloan realized the need to differentiate long-term thinking from the daily operations of management and of creating a policy for objectives projected in a desirable future. Studying the managerial performance of Sloan at General Motors, and of other top managers during the dominance of industrial corporations, Chandler (1962, p. 13) defined strategy as "the determination of the basic, long-term goals and objectives of an enterprise, and the adoption of a course of action and the allocation of resources necessary for those goals." Chandler analyzed the relationship between strategy design and the structure of the firm, and how to optimize that structure to support long-term managerial thinking and decision-making. The answer for the specific conditions of that time was to differentiate between top management's responsibility to design the firm's strategy and operational management's responsibility to implement that strategy.

A significant contributor to the classical strategy was Kenneth Andrews (1971), who explained the need for a strategic internal analysis of the firm to identify its strengths and weaknesses, and a strategic external analysis of the business environment to discover the opportunities for and threats to the firm's performance. While the strengths and weaknesses of the firm can be obtained objectively as a result of rational analysis, discovering the opportunities and threats in the external environment is a result of managers' subjective appraisal. However, deliberate strategies can be designed for a predictable future and based on rational economic analyses (Dess et al., 2018; Johnson et al., 2017; Rumelt, 2012).

A new wave of the strategy design came with the contributions of Michael Porter on competitive advantage in the external business environment (Porter, 1980, 1985). Porter introduces new concepts and instruments to the competitive business environment. Porter's model of competitive analysis contains five fundamental generic forces acting in the external business environment that influence the competition and contribute to success or failure in achieving a competitive advantage. Understanding the dynamics of these forces and acting on them in accordance with internal strengths and weaknesses are the necessary conditions for designing the firm's strategies. In Porter's view, "Competitive strategy is the search for a favorable competitive position in an industry, the fundamental arena in which competition occurs. The competitive strategy aims to establish a profitable and sustainable position against the forces that determine industry competition" (Porter, 1985, p. 1).

The five forces that determine the economic behavior of a firm in a competitive industry are the threat of new entrants, the bargaining power of suppliers, the bargaining power of buyers, the threat of substitute products or services, and the rivalry among existing firms. New entrants are potential competitors, and if they decide to enter the market, the pressure of the competition will increase. The threat of the new entrants depends mostly on the economy of scale, brand identity, switching costs, capital requirements, access to distribution channels, government policies, and expected retaliation. The incumbent firms conceive of creating some barriers to discourage potential entrants from making the decision to enter the market. The bargaining power of suppliers depends on supplier concentration, the importance of purchasing volume for the supplier, the presence of substitute products, switching costs, and the probability of creating backward integration by firms in that specific industry. The firm is, at the same time, a buyer and a supplier. Thus, the threat of the bargaining power of the supplier is somehow symmetrical with that of the buyer. For both of them, we should add the role of knowledge distribution between the firm, the supplier, and the buyer. The threat of substitutes depends on the rate of innovation in that specific industry, the switching costs, the buyer's readiness for change to new products and services, and the relative price performance of substitutes. Porter's model uses an economic metric to measure the impact of each force and the profitability of each possible strategy.

Based on the five forces model, Porter (1985) defines three generic strategies firms can use to achieve a *sustainable competitive advantage*. These generic strategies are the cost leadership strategy, the differentiation strategy, and the focus strategy. The last one has two versions: cost focus and differentiation focus. The cost leadership and differentiation strategies can be designed for a large market spectrum, while the focus strategy is addressed to a market segment. As Porter (1985, p. 11) emphasizes, "Each of the generic strategies involves a fundamentally different route to competitive advantage, combining a choice about the type of competitive advantage sought with the scope of a strategic target in which competitive advantage is to be achieved."

In the *cost leadership strategy,* the firm tries to become the low-cost producer in its industry. The design follows economic metrics and the experience curve in dealing with new technologies or procedures closely. The strategy aims to perform above the average of all firms in that specific industry, at that specific time. Cost leadership can be developed when there is an economy of scale supported by mass production. The *differentiation strategy* is used when mass production is replaced by a smaller production output or when the firm delivers services. The key concept behind this strategy is *uniqueness*. This strategy is driven by the psychological needs of buyers to get products and services that have unique features. Being enthusiastic about the fact nobody else owns such products or benefits from such services, the user is willing to pay a premium price. The *focus strategy* is designed for one or several segments of the market that can be controlled by the firm. Within that segment, the firm can apply the principles of the low-cost strategy, or those that define the differentiation strategy.

The evolutionary strategy approach. The evolutionary strategy is based on the emergent perception of time and the profit-maximization principle. Time is no longer stationary, but moving. The future comes to us, and we react to all the events that influence the decision-making process in the firm. The perception of uncertainty about future events is much higher than in the previous case, and that makes the long-term solutions of top managers more difficult and less successful. At the same time, markets impose fierce competition for survival that can be understood in terms of Darwin's theory of natural selection. Markets are more powerful than managers in selecting winners and losers. Managers should change their focus from elaborating grand strategies to finding the best ways to adapt to market requirements. This switch implies replacing the rational and deliberate approach with probabilistic thinking based on market distributions of events.

Bruce Henderson, the founder of the well-known Boston Consulting Group (BCG), considers classical economic theories and deliberate strategies to be too abstract to yield practical solutions for firms in their struggle for survival. Instead, Darwin's theory of natural selection could be a better model. He states: "Human beings may be at the top of the ecological chain, but we are still members of the ecological community. That is why Darwin is probably a better guide to business competition than economists are" (Henderson, 1989, p. 143). The evolutionists promote a reactive attitude of firms in a changeable market and deny the use of deliberate strategies. They reduce the whole strategy design to the adaptation process, which can never be a good strategy for first-mover firms.

The processual strategy approach. As a general characteristic, the processual strategy model continues the critique of deliberate strategy design and encourages the probabilistic thinking and the emergent process approach. Whittington (2001, p. 21) remarks that "the best Processual advice is not to strive after the unattainable ideal of rational fluid action, but to accept and work with the world as it is." In this perspective, researchers consider that in any organization, strategy design should not remain a task of only the top managers, but should involve in different forms all the employees. Organizational behavior matters in the strategy design because it influences the implementation of any strategy. Thus, the processual approach integrates both the conceptual phase of strategy design and the action of its implementation. If the design phase may benefit from deliberate input, the implementation phase depends on the emergent time perception. Downgrading the role of rationality to bounded rationality (Güth & Kliemt, 2017; Simon, 1979, 2000), the processual strategy design reflects much better the state of knowledge about the firm and the environment, and therefore about the possible future.

The promoters of the processual strategy design put their emphasis on the internal resources of the firm, and not on the probable opportunities in the market. They underline the fundamental role of tangible and intangible resources and of the core competencies in designing strategies for a sustainable competitive advantage (Barney & Clark, 2007; Grant, 1991, 1997; Hamel & Prahalad, 1994).

The systemic strategy approach. For Whittington (2001), the systemic strategy approach is the most complex, since strategy design is not abstract conceptual work but a very practical way to contribute to the growth of the firm and to enhance its competitiveness in a global market (Aoki, 1996; Mellahi et al., 2005; Song & Lee, 2014). Thus, systemic theorists reconsider the input to the deliberate strategy design and integrate it into the overall perspective of the economic, social, political, and cultural environment. The decision-makers and strategists are not living and thinking in pure economic environments, and they do not construct their decisions based only on profit-maximization and efficiency theory. They are embedded in real organizations, which are integrated into complex social systems. Thus, the systemic perspective on strategy uses systems thinking (Jackson, 2019; Senge, 1999), and it aggregates all factors that contribute to the firm's growth and competitiveness. The classical strategy approach was developed in the American economy and culture, and that explains why it is incorporated into most textbooks on strategies. However, when it is implemented in countries with emergent economies or in those with totally different cultures, the results cannot match the performance of American firms. The systemic strategy approach is culturally dependent and reflects much better the needs of different socioeconomic communities. "Important, therefore, to the systemic theory are differences between countries' social systems and changes within countries' social systems" (Whittington, 2001, p. 27). In each country, there is a specific combination of firms, family businesses, entrepreneurship, markets, legislation, culture, religion, banks, and government policies. That combination sets up the background for the strategy design and its specific implementation. Also, the perception of the future depends on these kinds of possible combinations. Consider a spectrum where a deterministic approach like that of the Islamic religion is on one end, and probabilistic thinking as in free-market competition is on the other. Between them is a broad range of possible approaches to strategy design.

Although the five forces in Porter's model of competitive advantage analysis are included in almost any book on strategy, their application in countries with different relationships between firms, banks, markets, and government agencies is constrained to each specific industry configuration. For instance, in Japan, there is an implicit relationship between a firm and its main bank. Also, in Japan, there are different corporate groups, with the generic name of *keiretsu*, that have very complicated power structures. However, the concept of *keiretsu* is fuzzy because there are no explicit relationships between firms, banks, and governmental agencies, and no clear boundaries between those corporate groups. "A firm usually has a bank that is its largest lender, one of its largest shareholders, and sometimes supplies one or two board members. The bank, in this case, is called the 'main bank' of the firm" (Hoshi, 1996, p. 285). Another important financial aspect of Japanese firms is cross-stockholding, a phenomenon that contributes substantially to creating corporate systems, which are mutually interconnected and "supported by a distinct institutional mix" (Aoki, 1996, p. 33).

In Europe, there are many differences between the classical strategy approach and the systemic approach of the Germanic economies – Germany, Austria, and Switzerland – where banks and other financial institutions, together with the government, play important roles in long-term decision-making (Whittington, 2001). Similar relationships in the Netherlands and the Scandinavian countries are not as strong as in the Germanic countries.

In conclusion, Whittington (2001, p. 37) states that the systemic strategy approach challenges "the universality of any single model of strategy. The objectives of the strategy and the models of strategy-making depend on the strategists' social characteristics and the social context in which they operate."

4.2.2 The Schools of Strategy Design

From the literature on different schools of thought about strategy, we selected the excellent synthesis of Mintzberg, Ahlstrand, and Lampel (1998), *Strategy Safari: The Complete Guide through the Wilds of Strategic Management,* for its comprehensiveness and semantic structure. The book presents ten major schools of strategic thinking and strategy design. These schools have many characteristics already found in the Whittington (2001) ontology, but the originality of *Strategy Safari* cannot be ignored by making a simple correspondence between the four classes of strategies considered by Whittington (2001) and these ten schools of strategic thinking explored in detail by Mintzberg et al. (1998): 1) the design school; 2) the planning school; 3) the positioning school; 4) the entrepreneurial school; 5) the cognitive school; 6) the learning school; 7) the power school; 8) the cultural school; 9) the environmental school; and 10) the configuration school. In the following sections, we present the most distinctive features of each school and how the school influences the managers' strategy design.

The design school: Strategy formation as a process of conception. Mintzberg et al. (1998, p. 24) observe, "The design school represents, without question, the most influential view of the strategy-formation process. Its key concepts continue to form the base of undergraduate and MBA strategy courses as well as a great deal of the practice of strategic management." This school stresses the strategic analysis of the internal and external business environment (Hill & Jones, 1998; Thompson & Strickland, 2001; Wheelen & Hunger, 2004). The internal analysis identifies the strengths and weaknesses of the firm, and the external analysis identifies possible opportunities and threats for the future development of the firm. The findings of all these analyses are structured into the well-known SWOT (strengths, weaknesses, opportunities, and threats) framework. The basic idea of this strategy design is to use the firms' strengths to chase business opportunities and reduce the pressure of potential threats. In a more advanced analysis, Spender and Strong (2014) integrate a firm's business model and the results of internal and external analyses into a pattern that defines the firm's *opportunity space*. The defining factors of this opportunity space are specific to each firm, and they are in a continuous dynamic: "These factors are never exactly the same for any two companies, so each business model is unique, and this is why managers sense their firms are different. Everything in this equation is dynamic and constantly changing, and so with it the business model" (Spender & Strong, 2014, p. 10). Strategy in the design school is the result of a deliberate process of conscious thought, and from this point of view, it belongs to the classical strategy design of Whittington's framework (2001).

The planning school: Strategy formation as a formal process. Planning means well-defined objectives, resource allocation, plans, and deadlines for achieving those objectives. It is based on the deterministic and linear thinking models (Bratianu, 2015b; Ohmae, 1982), quantitative methods, and economic metrics for the evaluation of all kinds of numerical indicators. Basically, the analysts "take the SWOT model, divide it into neatly delineated steps, articulate each of these with lots of checklists and techniques, and give special attention to the setting of objectives on the front end and the elaboration of budgets and operating plans on the back end" (Mintzberg et al., 1998, p. 49). Thus, quantitative analysis becomes more important than the qualitative interpretation of trends and the needs that must be met. Although numbers sometimes have an impressive power in the decision-making process, extrapolating from the thinking used for operational planning to strategic planning leads to an inherent weakness in anticipating the future. The planning school evolved from the classical command-and-control managerial philosophy since a plan also constitutes the reference used to control the final result. The magic of numbers for some managers turns out to be a real obstacle for others since they hide the complexity of managing uncertainty. The main assumption of these planners, that the future can be anticipated because the external environment evolves according to some mathematical models, is a major fallacy of strategic planning (Mintzberg, 2000; Mintzberg et al., 1998; Warren, 2008).

The positioning school: Strategy formation as an analytical process. Although it is hard to find a specific date for the birth of a school of strategy, for the positioning school Mintzberg et al. (1998) consider that "the watershed year was 1980, when Michael Porter published *Competitive strategy*." The book had the effect of stimulating a new direction of research and of publishing many other books and papers on that topic. The positioning school continues the tradition of the design and planning schools in considering the manager's competence in anticipating the future and designing strategies for achieving some defined objectives. The new ideas revealed by Porter can be synthesized as follows:

- The external environment is practically infinite in its variety and space in comparison with the internal business environment. That makes its analysis by using one single method or model very difficult. The solution is to structure it into several layers and for each layer to use a different tool for analysis.
- Metaphorically, that is the solution found in fluid mechanics in studying the resistant forces to the motion of a ship on the seawater. Having an aerospace engineering background, Porter knew the boundary-layer theory and focused his analysis on the industry layer where the pressure of competition is very high. Porter (1980) developed the five forces model and the value chain analysis model to study the necessary conditions for achieving competitive advantage.
- While in the design and planning schools there are no limits on how many strategies can be formulated, Porter (1980) shows that the number of strategies should be limited as a result of constrained resources and managerial capability of implementing them. He defined three generic strategies, which we presented in the previous section: cost leadership, differentiation, and focus strategies. The aim of those strategies is to achieve sustainable competitive advantage and, as a consequence, to get a favorable position in the market.

It is interesting to note that the positioning school has many similar ideas to those used in battles and wars (Clausewitz, 1989; Kaufman, 1994; Sun Tzu, 1971). Great military strategies from Alexander to Napoleon were designed by breaking traditional thinking and creating unexpected battlefield dynamics (Bose, 2004; Mintzberg et al., 1998).

The entrepreneurial school: Strategy formation as a visionary process. This school embraces both deliberate and emergent aspects of strategy formation. It is deliberate since it is based on rational knowledge and some economic analytics, and it is emergent since entrepreneurs are using their intuition and imagination to deal with the absence of knowledge yet look toward the future. "The most central concept of this school is *vision*, a mental representation of strategy, created or at least expressed in the head of the leader" (Mintzberg et al., 1998, p. 124). Vision is not based on logic or economic analyses but on the intuitive power of the entrepreneur. Richard Branson, the famous architect of the business conglomerate Virgin, recognizes this inner power of the entrepreneur: "Most of what I have done with the Virgin Group is about my own gut instinct. I've never analyzed what I do in any formal way. What would be the point? In business, as in life, you never step into the same river twice" (Branson, 2009, p. 6).

Although the entrepreneurial school was born in the economic thinking context, it moved progressively toward the business challenges of searching for opportunities and new ways of creating wealth. One of the key contributors to the entrepreneurial school was Joseph Schumpeter, who defined the powerful concept of *creative destruction* (Schumpeter, 1950). Creative destruction is the driving force of innovation and entrepreneurship. For Schumpeter, the entrepreneur is the individual whose inspiration finds the new business idea. Thus, the emphasis is not on the investment or the risks taken but on the new business idea. Putting existing technological elements and procedures together in a new way or structure may lead to a new business idea. For instance, Steve Jobs had the idea of integrating three different technologies (i.e., communication, computing, and the Internet) into one single device he called the iPhone. That was a disruptive business idea supported by a disruptive technology (Isaacson, 2011; Kahney, 2008; Segall, 2012). In contrast to Schumpeter, Knight (2006) emphasizes the risk the entrepreneur is taking when he initiates a new business, and the uncertainty is high.

The cognitive school: Strategy formation as a mental process. According to Mintzberg et al. (1998), the main premises of this school in development are the following:

1) Strategy formation is a cognitive process that takes place in the mind of the strategist.
2) Strategies thus emerge as perspectives – in the forms of concepts, maps, schemas, and frames – that shape how people deal with inputs from the environment.
3) The seen world, in other words, can be modeled, it can be framed, and it can be constructed. (Mintzberg et al., 1998, p. 170)

The emphasis in this school is on the cognitive power of shaping the future through new concepts, ideas, and models. Managers who already have a series of knowledge maps about the present situation of the firm can advance new ideas about its further development. However, mental work is not solely rational. Cognition is influenced significantly by emotion (Damasio, 2003, 2012; Hill, 2008; LeDoux, 1999; Nussbaum, 2001), and thus strategy design should integrate the two components (Kotter, 1996; Mintzberg et al., 1998; Nonaka & Zhu, 2012).

We consider that all strategy designs represent cognitive processes and that it is not relevant at all to define a specific school focusing on cognition. We understand the need of Mintzberg et al. (1998) to reveal how important conceptual work is in designing a strategy, but that is implicit in any kind of strategy design.

The learning school: Strategy formation as an emergent process. The business environment is changing continuously, with different intensities. Change creates new contexts and reveals new phenomena with respect to the moment of designing the strategy. Thus, managers have to learn about them and adapt the strategy to the new situation. The strategy design is not a deliberate one for a static environment anymore. It is open to incorporating new ideas and adapting to new conditions, as a result of individual and organizational learning (Argote, 2013; North & Kumta, 2018; Rother, 2010).

Learning is an active process that happens as a result of seeing the future coming toward us with its uncertainty and new experiences. Being open to change, the strategy design is flexible and capable of restructuring such that the knowledge learned can be incorporated into the initial design, contributing directly to its improvement. The emergence of the future intensifies knowledge dynamics (Bratianu, 2016) at the interface between action and reflection, and generates new ideas, which are incorporated into the strategy design. Quinn (1980) analyzes this process and concludes that it evolves incrementally, as in *logical incrementalism*. "The real strategy tends to evolve as internal decisions and external events flow together to create a new, widely shared consensus for action among key members of the top-management team. In well-run organizations, managers pro-actively guide these streams of actions and events incrementally toward conscious strategies" (Quinn, 1980, p. 15).

A classic example of logical incrementalism is the *Toyota system* of continuous improvement based on the well-known PDCA (Plan–Do–Check–Act) cycle (Rother, 2010). *Plan* is the first phase of the cycle, in which the manager defines a target condition and the working hypothesis. *Do* is the action of testing the working hypothesis, carried out on a small scale. *Check* is the phase of comparing the result of an action with the expected outcome. *Act* may have two components: first, to stabilize what is working well, and second, to change what did not work. Then, the whole cycle starts again until the target condition is achieved. When it adopted this incremental improvement method, Toyota added the request to *go and see* what actually happens on the shop floor. The PDCA cycle served as an inspiration for Nonaka (1994) and Nonaka and Takeuchi (1995) in their design of the *knowledge spiral* as a driving force of the knowledge creation dynamic model.

The power school: Strategy formation as a process of negotiation. In any organization, there is a distribution of power in decision-making and strategy design. The power school focuses on this power distribution. If there is autocratic management, strategies are designed by the top managers only and then implemented by middle and line managers. It is a well-defined top-down process. In a democratic managerial environment, decisions result from many debates and negotiations between different groups of interests, which reflect social interaction and shared beliefs and values. The power school distinguishes between micropolitics, as an internal phenomenon, and macropolitics, when negotiations occur between organizations in the external environment. Politics is generated by the nonuniform distribution of power, competition for resources, and goal-setting at the level of teams, departments, and the whole organization. Because there are negotiations over designing goals and strategies, which reflect the interests of different groups, strategizing cannot lead to optimal processes. Strategy designs are more emergent than deliberate and more focused on economic metrics than on perspectives.

The cultural school: Strategy formation as a collective process. Organizational culture is a result of an integration process, and it acts somehow in opposition to power. While power strategies aim for change, culture strategies aim for stability and maintaining the status quo. Organizational culture behaves like a collective cognition. The cultural contribution in strategy design was demonstrated by Japanese managers, since culture plays an important role in strategy design in Japanese firms (Nonaka & Takeuchi, 1995; Ohmae, 1982). Culture incorporates beliefs, values, and traditions. Organizational culture, therefore, acts as a filter to interpret all the information and knowledge in an organization and feed the cognitive strategy design. The cultural school focuses on social interaction and shared beliefs and values, as well as on the dominant logic in decision-making. Because of its inertial force, organizational culture does not encourage "strategic change so much as the perpetuation of existing strategy; at best, it tends to promote shifts in position within the organization's overall strategic perspective" (Mintzberg et al., 1998, p. 268).

The environmental school: Strategy formation as a reactive process. This school focuses on the active role played by the environment as a driving force of change in strategy design. If all the other schools consider managers and the organization as the only active participants in strategy design, this school gives importance to the external environment and its forces for change. The organization becomes a reactive force and can respond with emergent strategies. The environmental school developed from the contingency theory of management, which studies the dynamics between organizations and their environment. We consider that this school exaggerates in offering the primordial role to external forces and letting the organization adapt passively to external changes. In fact, the environment is composed of all the other organizations, regardless of whether they are profit making or not, and among them there are many innovative firms. These innovative firms have demonstrated that they can change the world with their disruptive technologies and business innovations.

The configuration school: Strategy formation as a process of transformation. Configuration is a concept that reflects the structure of a certain system or system of systems. Reductionism simplifies the complexity of the real world, leading many of us to focus only on a certain firm, or the firm and its associated market. But in their vision of the future, managers should consider the configuration of a larger environment, and they should anticipate the possible changes that will come in the future. All of those changes will bring forth a series of transformations of the initial configuration. The world is changing, and the firm must change together with the whole system. "The key to strategic management, therefore, is to sustain stability or at least adaptable strategic change most of the time, but periodically to recognize the need for transformation and be able to manage that disruptive process without destroying the organization" (Mintzberg et al., 1998, p. 305).

5 Generic Knowledge Strategies

5.1 The Known-Unknowns Dynamics

The concept of *generic strategies* was introduced into strategic thinking by Michael Porter in his seminal book *Competitive Advantage: Creating and Sustaining Superior Performance* (1985), which was discussed in the previous section. *Generic knowledge strategies* refer to those knowledge strategies that can be designed and implemented in any organization in accordance with the needs and dynamic capabilities of that organization. Because of the intangibility of knowledge resources and their nonlinearity, Porter's generic strategies cannot be extended directly to the knowledge domain (Bolisani & Bratianu, 2018; Grant, 1996; Spender, 1996; Sveiby, 2001). They should be viewed from a different perspective. There are two such perspectives: a) the organizational knowledge dynamics (Bratianu et al., 2011), and b) the known-unknowns matrix (Dalkir, 2005). The organizational knowledge dynamics (OKD) model is based on the systems thinking (Jackson, 2019) approach. The purpose of such an analysis is to identify the main variables that influence the knowledge-level dynamics in the organization and to see how we can control them in a strategic perspective. These variables are knowledge creation, knowledge acquisition, knowledge loss, knowledge transfer through the interface of the system, and knowledge sharing. We shall discuss these variables when we analyze each type of knowledge strategy. The story with the *known-unknowns* paradox is related to the answer given by the former Secretary of Defense Donald Rumsfeld during a press briefing:

> Reports that say that something hasn't happened are always interesting to me, because as we know, there are *known-knowns*; there are things we know we know. We also know there are *known-unknowns*; that is to say, we know there are some things we do not know. But there are also *unknown-unknowns*—the ones we don't know we don't know. (Rumsfeld, 2002; italics added)

The *known-unknowns* matrix (Dalkir, 2005) is a generalized framework of that discussion, structuring the tension between what is known and what could be known regarding a problem or situation. Figure 2 illustrates the knowledge states of the system and the associated strategies aimed at providing the knowledge resources for achieving a sustainable competitive advantage for the firm. These knowledge states contain both explicit and tacit knowledge. Since explicit knowledge is rational and a product of the conscious zone of the brain, we know how much we know regarding a problem. However, tacit knowledge is managed by the cognitive unconscious (Damasio, 2012; Lakoff & Johnson, 1999), and for us, it is almost impossible to know how much we know. We know about our experiences and lessons learned from them, but we cannot know all the tacit knowledge we may dispose of at a given time. For us, this tacit knowledge is a kind of *known-unknown*. Beyond tacit knowledge considered as a conscious unknown, it is also the absence of knowledge as unknown in the external world, especially when we discuss the future and its uncertainty.

In a finite world of knowledge and deterministic thinking, *known-unknowns* represent the knowledge domain we know, and we can make use of it. Most of this domain results from the formal education we get in schools and universities, and it is the rational view of the external world. It is

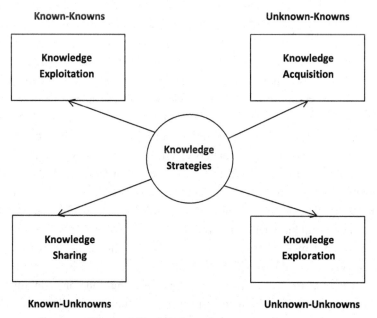

Figure 2 Generic knowledge strategies

the interpretation of the metaphor used to explain how our brain is like a container where knowledge is accumulated through learning. "The idea of knowledge as the contents of a mental filing cabinet is, I believe, the most stultifying conception in educational thought. But it has been shared by all major combatants in the educational debates of this century" (Bereiter, 2002, p. 24). Since the container has a finite volume, we know how much of it is full at any time. If we consider a finite knowledge domain – and we already know a good part of it – then we are aware of what we don't know. For us that represents the *unknown-knowns*; that is, knowledge we don't have at a given time but which we can acquire. Both concepts *known-knowns* and *unknown-knowns* reflect explicit knowledge, which is rational and conscious knowledge; we are aware of it. The next concepts, *known-unknowns*, and *unknown-unknowns*, consider both explicit and tacit forms of knowledge, or the triad composed of rational, emotional, and spiritual knowledge (Bratianu & Bejinaru, 2019). Since tacit knowledge is gained through direct experience and is processed by our cognitive unconscious, we know that we acquired some knowledge, but we do not know how much. That is the meaning of the concept *known-unknowns*. When we think about the future and its absence of knowledge (Spender, 2014), we have to admit that there could be many events we cannot anticipate, which represent for us *unknowns-unknowns*.

When individuals' knowledge is integrated into organizational knowledge (Bratianu, 2013, 2015a), all the arguments above can be scaled up to the level of the organization. The *known-knowns* represent, in this case, all the knowledge that is embedded in the organizational structure, procedures, regulations, intellectual propriety rights, and knowledge maps, where they exist. Managers know what kind of knowledge and approximately how much, by comparison with certain standards, they have in the organization. It is the knowledge they can count on and use extensively. For such a situation, the best strategy managers can design is *knowledge exploitation*. When the firm does not have the knowledge resources necessary for the adaptation of development – the *unknown-knowns* they need – it is recommended that they adopt the strategy of *knowledge acquisition*. Tacit knowledge is personal knowledge and very difficult to evaluate at the level of the organization. However, as managerial practice has shown, there are methods to discover this hidden experiential knowledge (Kolb, 2015), or *known-unknowns*, and to use it in organizational learning and for changing the knowledge distribution in the organization. For such a case, the *knowledge sharing strategy design* is recommended. Finally, when the firm would like to pursue an innovation strategy, and knowledge absence (Spender, 2014) becomes a dominant variable, there are many *unknown-unknowns*, and the best strategy managers can design is *the knowledge exploration* strategy. Each of these four main types of generic knowledge strategy will be discussed in the following sections.

5.2 The Strategy of Knowledge Exploitation

5.2.1 Organizational Nonlinear Integrators

Knowledge is a strategic resource, but it is created and owned by individuals (Davenport & Prusak, 2000; Polanyi, 1962, 1983; Russell, 2009). In organizations, knowledge can be integrated and structured to produce collective knowledge known as *organizational knowledge*. In the literature, we find two meanings associated with this concept. The *restrictive* meaning refers to organizational knowledge owned by the organization. It is the knowledge embedded in regulations, working procedures, intellectual property rights, organizational culture, databases, and software systems. Edvinsson (2002) used to say that it is the knowledge that remains in an organization when all the employees have left for home. It is owned and controlled by the organization. *Extensive* organizational knowledge refers to the entire field of knowledge, including the knowledge owned by employees. For knowledge-intensive organizations, organizational knowledge in all its forms constitutes a strategic resource (Brown & Duguid, 1998).

The knowledge of individuals is integrated into organizational knowledge by *organizational integrators*: technology, managers, leaders, and organizational culture. Technology introduces specific working structures in which individuals are aggregated to perform complex activities. The simplest form of such aggregation is the classical assembly line created by Henry Ford in the car industry. The assembly line is a *linear integrator* since it aggregates workers according to a linear sequence of tasks dictated by a specific procedure. An IT system can be a nonlinear integrator, since it allows workers to perform different tasks with different contributions to the final product or service. Managers, leaders, and organizational culture are *nonlinear integrators* (Bratianu, 2013) because they create working structures where knowledge is integrated into all its forms (i.e., rational, emotional, and spiritual). Integrated knowledge, together with some other intangibles, constitutes at the organizational level the intellectual capital of the firm (Andriessen, 2004; Ricceri, 2008).

Nonaka and Takeuchi (1995) show that knowledge is created at the individual level and amplified at the team and organizational levels through social interaction and two specific processes: *socialization* when the exchange of tacit knowledge is dominant, and *combination* when explicit knowledge is dominant. During these social interactions, knowledge is created and increased in a spiral, following a nonlinear pattern. The strategy of knowledge exploitation is focused on the visible part of organizational knowledge and uses it efficiently to achieve the organization's objectives. As March (1991, p. 71) emphasizes, "Exploitation includes such things as refinement, choice, production, efficiency, selection, implementation, execution." Although we discuss knowledge exploitation and knowledge exploration as generic strategies separately, in practice, many firms use them in combination. Some authors call this ability to combine these strategies *the quality of organizational ambidexterity* (Andriopoulos & Lewis, 2009; Raisch et al., 2009).

5.2.2 Knowledge Codification

Codification is a process of transforming raw data, information, and knowledge into messages that can be communicated using *codes*. The most used code is natural language. It allows us to transform our experience, stored as tacit knowledge, into explicit knowledge, which can be communicated and embedded into documents and databases. In multinational companies, where workers are from different countries and speak different languages, there is always a language that plays a dominant role in communication and is the communication code for explicit knowledge.

The codification process is fundamental for knowledge exploitation. "Knowledge codification implies transforming cognitive, emotional, and spiritual knowledge into messages that can be understood by all employees of a certain organization. It occurs inside the organization, but its consequences should be observed in both internal and external environments" (Bolisani & Bratianu, 2018, p. 153). Knowledge codification is essential not only in social interactions but also in the interaction between workers and technology since all procedures are the result of knowledge codification.

Although most writers refer to the codification of data, information, and rational knowledge, it is useful to note that emotional knowledge and spiritual knowledge also are forms of knowledge that can be codified in an organization. For instance, many firms have dress codes which incorporate predominantly emotional knowledge and spiritual knowledge. Dress codes vary from imposing strict uniforms (as for the police, hospitals, armies, and some specific laboratories) to business casual, or casual. Dress codes incorporate rational, emotional, and spiritual knowledge in different combinations and proportions. For instance, in hospitals, doctors and nurses have white clothes that reflect both rational and emotional knowledge, while in universities during specific ceremonies, professors and students wear caps and gowns of different designs and colors, which reflect both emotional and spiritual knowledge.

A deep codification in many firms is their *ethical code*. According to *Collins English Dictionary*, an ethical code is "a set of moral principles used to govern the conduct of a profession." For example, the ethical code that its founder gave to IBM contains the following requirements (Gerstner, 2003, p. 184):

- Excellence in everything we do.
- Superior customer service.
- Respect for the individual.

Samsung's ethical code is structured as a "Trinity of Values," which comprises management philosophy, core values, and business principles (Song & Lee, 2014, p. 111). It is interesting to note that in these business principles, there is no focus on profit or shareholders' interest in maximizing that profit. It is implicitly assumed that if Samsung applies those principles, then profit will be the normal outcome. These generic formulations are detailed in a further series of conduct rules for all employees. "Samsung has set forth core items that were to be followed by all employees as its management principles. The company has 5 overarching principles, 15 detailed principles, and 42 conduct rules that its employees are expected to follow" (Song & Lee, 2014, p. 111).

5.2.3 Knowledge Mapping

The knowledge exploitation strategy can be successful if managers are aware of the *known-knowns* in the organization, which means knowing the available knowledge in all its forms and its distribution throughout the organization. Unfortunately, at this time there is not a unique and valid metric for individual knowledge or organizational knowledge, although there are some suggestions (Andriessen, 2004; Bolisani & Oltramari, 2012; Guthrie et al., 2012; Sveiby, 2010; Vallejo-Alonso et al., 2011).

The best way for managers to learn about the distribution of knowledge in the organization is to create knowledge maps. These are navigational tools for managers to use and reuse to understand their organization's knowledge. "A knowledge map portrays the sources, flows, constraints, and sinks (losses or stopping points) of knowledge within an organization" (Liebowitz, 2005, p. 77). A knowledge map results from a knowledge audit, which focuses on:

- what knowledge exists in a part of the whole organization, and what knowledge is missing regarding managers' expectations
- evaluation of the relative densities of knowledge in the mapped area
- evaluations of the knowledge flows or fluxes between the main interest points
- what constraints prevent optimizing the knowledge flows in the organization.

Based on these graphical illustrations, managers can understand much better the organizational knowledge dynamics and provide solutions for knowledge bottlenecks and knowledge losses. Kudryavtsev and Gavrilova (2017) show that there are different types of maps and diagrams for knowledge representations, and managers should use them according to their purpose. There are maps for operational knowledge management and maps for strategic knowledge management, each with specific elements and time frameworks.

Managers can use software tools and artificial intelligence applications to construct knowledge maps. Knowledge maps represent in a simplified way how the fields of knowledge are structured in the organization. These structures can be hierarchical or neural. In the first case, the search for a certain piece of knowledge is performed top-down, sequence by sequence; in the second case, the search uses an algorithm to find the knowledge needed in a shorter time. The first mapping system uses linear logic, while the second uses a nonlinear logic. From a cognitivist perspective, a *knowledge map* represents an extension of a *mind map* (Buzan & Buzan, 1993). The value of a knowledge map is its power to illustrate the knowledge distribution in an organization and the algorithms it uses to find the needed spot of knowledge easily.

More advanced knowledge maps are based on the metaphor *stocks-and-flows*. A stocks-and-flows knowledge map represents the sources of knowledge (its stocks) in the organization's nodes and knowledge flows as links between nodes (Kim et al., 2003). Such a map can also show the constraints of knowledge flows, which is a good starting point for improving the knowledge exploitation strategy.

5.3 The Strategy of Knowledge Acquisition

5.3.1 Knowledge Acquisition

The *known-unknowns* state of knowledge occurs when we know what we know, and by comparing it to a certain knowledge standard or performance, we reveal what we do not know yet. The knowledge gap between what we know and what we should know can be reduced or eliminated by knowledge acquisition (Bratianu, 2015a; Zack, 1999). Knowledge acquisition means purchasing knowledge from some external sources or obtaining it in a network exchange. Knowledge acquisition is used as an alternative to knowledge creation when a firm does not have enough potential to generate the knowledge it needs internally through research (Chaston & Mangles, 2000; Hoe & McShane, 2010). Knowledge acquisition is used especially by SMEs when they do not have the time and/or the financial resources they need to develop their own knowledge (Chan & Chao, 2008; Durst & Edvardson, 2012). Knowledge acquisition refers mostly to rational knowledge since emotional and spiritual knowledge can be generated internally.

Knowledge acquisition can occur in a variety of forms: purchasing research journals and international databases, purchasing software and artificial intelligence applications, purchasing training programs and expertise from consultancy firms, getting knowledge in network exchange arrangements, and hiring experts with rich experience and expertise. In a larger perspective, knowledge acquisition represents the knowledge that crosses the interface with the external business environment (Liao et al., 2010). For entrepreneurial firms, knowledge is usually acquired by purchasing intellectual property rights representing patents to implement new technologies for realizing new products and services. For small firms, it is recommended to enter *learning networks* to benefit from the knowledge exchange process (Chaston & Mangles, 2000; Kodama, 2011). It is interesting to note that knowledge flows between firms in the network are based on rational knowledge, but during the negotiation phase, managers use mostly their emotional and spiritual knowledge. Also, we must emphasize that any network involves a convergence of business principles and cultural values, which reveals the importance of sharing spiritual knowledge with the network partners. When integration into a business network is not an option, firms may look for business alliances. Business alliances take many forms based on the interests of the partners. We refer here to those alliances where one of the main activities is knowledge sharing (Tsai, 2001). The success of knowledge acquisition depends on the *absorptive capacity* of the firm (Cohen & Levinthal, 1990) and its dynamic capability (Teece, 2009).

In the literature, the knowledge acquisition strategy is also called the *knowledge capturing* process (Clark et al., 2008; Eucker, 2007; Milton, 2007). Knowledge capturing focuses on extracting valuable knowledge from experts and embedding that knowledge into databases and artificial intelligence applications. It is a very complex and specialized process designed to support the construction of *expert systems* and all kinds of artificial intelligence applications. Knowledge engineering aims at creating intelligent software programs, but the knowledge content of those programs must be obtained from experts, from their outstanding experience and their wisdom. Knowledge capturing must overcome some cognitive and personality barriers. It is difficult to extract the most significant knowledge from the experts' experience (Gladwell, 2008), and to convince experts to open their minds to that knowledge. Expert systems are software tools used by people in learning and decision-making (Milton, 2007).

More recently, in cognitive sciences, researchers discuss *Cognitive Task Analysis* (Clark et al., 2008) as a new activity domain for knowledge capturing.

5.3.2 Knowledge Retention

Knowledge retention is the process of applying the method of knowledge capturing to employees before they leave the firm. Many of them have valuable experience structured as tacit knowledge, which is multiplied many times when the number of employees leaving at the same time is very large. All this collective tacit knowledge can be lost if a large number of employees leave the organization and there is no strategy for knowledge retention. DeLong (2004) describes a knowledge catastrophe at Boeing when top management ignored the consequences of knowledge loss and had no knowledge retention strategy.

> After Boeing offered early retirement to 9,000 senior employees during a business downturn, an unexpected rush of new commercial airplane orders left the company critically short of skilled production workers. The knowledge lost from veteran employees combined with the inexperience of their replacements threw the firm's 737 and 747 assembly lines into chaos. (DeLong, 2004, p. 19)

Each organization possesses knowledge that is critical to its survival. To avoid the loss of such critical knowledge, top management should design a strategy to capture the knowledge of the leaving employees. This increases knowledge retention and reduces knowledge risks (Bratianu, 2018b; Durst, 2019; Durst & Zieba, 2017; Zieba & Durst, 2018). Knowledge retention can be achieved through different modes and by using different methods, such as intergenerational learning, knowledge recovery initiatives, and information technology applications to capture, store, and share knowledge (Agarwal & Islam, 2015; Bratianu & Leon, 2015; Martins & Meyer, 2012). Intergenerational knowledge transfer is efficient, especially in organizations that have an age layer structure, where knowledge sharing is less constrained. One good example is universities, where age layers are generated by the hierarchical structure and the traditional promotion systems (Lefter et al., 2011).

Intergenerational knowledge transfer becomes critical when business leaders retire, and there is the problem of transferring part of their experience to the new leaders. "Intelligent organizations create plans for leadership succession to make a slow and efficient transfer of knowledge from the leaders who retire towards the new generation of leaders. That means to develop a process of intergenerational learning and to create a necessary culture for making it efficient" (Tichy, 1997). Jack Welch is an excellent example of a leader who designed strategies for intergenerational knowledge transfer and the development of the next generation of leaders, including Jeff Immelt, who became the CEO of General Electric immediately after Welch retired.

5.4 The Strategy of Knowledge Sharing

5.4.1 Knowledge Sharing

Knowledge sharing is a generic expression used to designate the *voluntary* transfer of knowledge from one entity to another. The critical feature of knowledge sharing, which distinguishes it from the general activity of knowledge transfer, is the *willingness* of a certain entity to start that process (Davenport & Prusak, 2000; Hislop, 2005; Jashapara, 2011; North & Kumta, 2018). Entities can be individuals, teams, departments, and even organizations when discussing interorganizational knowledge sharing. The fundamental mechanism of knowledge sharing is the social interaction of people and their motivation in communicating with their peers. One of the most important outcomes of knowledge sharing is the formation of *organizational knowledge*, a basic construct used in knowledge management. The opposite of knowledge sharing is *knowledge hoarding*, which means that individuals are interested only in keeping their knowledge for themselves (Cyr & Choo, 2010; Nesheim & Gressgard, 2014; Reinholdt et al., 2011). Knowledge hoarding shows that people are afraid to share their experience with others in a competitive social environment, since they may put their hierarchical position in danger. "Typically, employees may not want to share what they know, fearing that once they share their specialized knowledge, they may not be needed" (Thatchenkery, 2005, p. 16). The balance between knowledge sharing and knowledge hoarding is strongly influenced by the organizational culture and the managerial philosophy concerning the balance between economic and social metrics. Figure 3 illustrates the tension between knowledge sharing by one individual and knowledge hoarding by the other, but it can be enlarged to groups of people. When competition is strong, both individuals A and B are afraid of sharing their knowledge since they may lose their hierarchical position. When there is a climate of cooperation, and knowledge sharing is stimulated and rewarded by the managers, both individuals A and B find knowledge sharing to be a good practice. These attitudes are symmetrical, and they lead toward a dynamic equilibrium. However, when one person has hidden his knowledge and takes advantage of the other person's knowledge, the situation is asymmetrical and induces a climate of frustration.

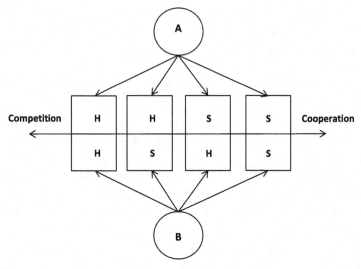

Figure 3 The knowledge sharing (S) – knowledge hoarding (H) dynamics

As Cyr and Choo (2010) observed, knowledge sharing as a social interaction process implies costs and benefits. The costs are not just financial since they also refer to the time and the mental effort of transforming tacit knowledge into explicit knowledge through externalization. Also, there is a certain codification effort involved in the communication process, especially when the receiving entity comprises individuals with different absorptive capacities. There should be a balance between those efforts and their benefits. In most situations, the rewards for knowledge sharing are not reduced to money or other material results. Professional appreciation and social recognition are more important than financial benefits.

Knowledge sharing can be a simple personal experience or a complex strategy designed to enhance organizational learning (Argote, 2013; Örtenblad, 2011; Rhem, 2017). "Knowledge sharing has been identified as a major focus area for knowledge management. The importance of this topic lies in the fact that it aims to link the individual level, where knowledge resides, and the organizational level, where knowledge is applied and attains value" (Sanchez et al., 2013). Closely related to knowledge sharing is *knowledge diffusion* (Braunerhjelm et al., 2010; Morone & Taylor, 2004). *Knowledge diffusion* is a metaphorical concept based on thermodynamics; it suggests that the propagation of knowledge in a social context is like the propagation of heat in a solid object from a region with a higher temperature toward a region with a lower temperature. In a similar way, knowledge about a specific domain or problem can be propagated from an individual or a team with a higher level of knowing toward a social region with a lower level of knowing. Bratianu (2015a) shows that thermodynamics also inspires us to introduce the concept of *knowledge convection*, which implies the motion of people with their embodied knowledge. Knowledge convection is closely related to knowledge flow, and it suggests the interaction between different knowledge fields in a certain social context. It is interesting to reflect also on the possible metaphorical construct of *knowledge radiation*, which implies a huge difference between the sender and the receiver of a message. That metaphor could be illustrated by the heat radiated from the sun to the earth. When a message becomes viral on the Internet, it is like a process of knowledge radiation, both in intensity and in propagation. A good understanding of knowledge diffusion, knowledge convection, and knowledge radiation could help managers to be more effective in the complex process of knowledge sharing.

In organizational knowledge dynamics, knowledge sharing does not contribute to knowledge creation, as some authors suggest. The contribution of knowledge sharing is an overall increase in the average level of organizational knowledge and a change in the distribution of knowledge. As a result, there is an increase in the organization's knowledge entropy with direct benefits for the innovation process (Bratianu, 2019). Thus, the knowledge sharing strategy creates conditions for stimulating innovations and increasing the knowledge absorptive capacity of the whole organization. The effectiveness of knowledge sharing depends not only on the level of knowing of the source but also on the level of knowing of the receiver. The higher the receiver's level of knowing, the more effective the process of knowledge sharing will be. This implies that knowledge sharing should sometimes be complemented by training programs to enhance the level of knowing (Reinholdt et al., 2011).

Among the newly developed methods to stimulate knowledge sharing in organizations is the *appreciative sharing of knowledge* (Thatchenkery, 2005). This method is based on the hypothesis that knowledge sharing is strongly influenced by organizational culture. As a result, knowledge sharing can be enhanced by building a corporate culture that encourages employees to share their experiences with others. At the same time, managers analyze the flows of knowledge and try to identify the potential barriers and bottlenecks in the real knowledge sharing process. For instance, Szulanski (1995, 1996, 2000), and Szulanski and Jensen (2004) extended the concept of *information stickiness* introduced by Hipel (1994) to *knowledge stickiness* to reveal the difficulties in knowledge sharing and transfer. "Knowledge transfer is seen as a process in which an organization recreates and maintains a complex, causally ambiguous set of routines in a new setting. Stickiness connotes difficulty experienced in that process" (Szulanski, 2000, p. 10).

Being a voluntary process supported by a positive motivation, knowledge sharing needs an organizational climate of *trust* (Castelfranchi & Falcone, 2010; Parra et al., 2011; Rousseau et al., 1998; Vanhala et al., 2011). If there is no trust in your colleagues, there is no motivation to share your experience with people who might envy you for your performance. According to Mayer et al. (1995, p. 712), trust is "the willingness of a party to be vulnerable to the actions of another party based on the expectation that the other will perform a particular action important to the trustor, irrespective of the ability to monitor or control that other party." The variable of vulnerability suggests that knowledge sharing might be a risky process in a very competitive social context. In conclusion, to design a knowledge sharing strategy means to provide solutions for developing a supportive organizational culture and a trustful psychological climate.

5.4.2 Communities of Practice

The idea of creating communities of practice is not new. We know that during the Middle Ages there were craft guilds composed of artisans willing to have professional structures for promoting their interests. These guilds created regulations and different procedures for coaching and knowledge sharing, such that young apprentices could learn the craft much better. Today, communities of practice come from individuals' willingness to belong to a formal or informal professional structure where they can share their knowledge and professional values. According to Wenger et al. (2002, p. 4), "Communities of practice are groups of people who share a concern, a set of problems, or a passion about a topic, and who deepen their knowledge and expertise in this area by interacting on an ongoing basis."

Members of such a community of practice can be from the same or from different organizations since they usually meet in their free time. Although traditionally members of a community of practice used to meet face-to-face to share their experience and work on common projects, today people's interactions happen mostly online. In the digital economy, communities of practice take full advantage of the Internet and all kinds of software applications for creating and sharing common databases and wiki projects. Since any community of practice implies a shared set of values, there is an ad hoc culture based on trust and social recognition, which stimulates knowledge sharing and knowledge co-creation. The concept of *practice* used in defining these communities refers to social practice. "Such a concept of practice includes both the explicit and the tacit. It includes what is said and what is left unsaid; what is represented and what is assumed" (Wenger, 1998, p. 47).

Individuals enter a community of practice with their full fields of rational, emotional, and spiritual knowledge. These individual knowledge fields integrate dynamically into the collective fields of knowledge generated by the whole community of practice. The feeling of belonging to a community of practice is generally a strong one, and it is the driving force for participating in such a community, where it is about knowledge sharing and learning. The main rule is the compatibility of members with a minimal set of values defined by the founders of the community of practice. That rule becomes very important when the community is open to people from different countries, with different cultures and religions. In communities of practice, the aim is cooperation, not competition. "As a result, there is an increase in members' commitment, motivation and interest in making their knowledge available for others. They also become aware of their capacity for accessing other individuals' knowledge" (Bratianu, 2015a, p. 276).

Being a social construct, a successful community of practice needs to satisfy a set of minimum requirements (Bolisani & Bratianu, 2018, p. 165):

- A well-defined *domain of knowledge sharing* that is attractive for a large spectrum of people.
- *A leader* able to create an attractive force, and a high level of social trust.
- *A critical mass* of participants willing to share their knowledge.
- *An agenda of events* which can be improved continuously.
- *A rewarding system* such that the most active participants feel that their efforts are appreciated by the other members of the community of practice.
- *A website, newsletter, or other publication.* These tools are important for creating a dynamic communication between all the members of that community of practice.

The leader is usually the founder of the community of practice, and is essential in designing the community and attracting people who are interested in sharing their knowledge. They are also the driving force in creating the critical mass of participants. Without such a force, it would be almost impossible to create that critical mass. In an online community of practice, the leader is less visible than in direct social interactions, but their strategy is embedded in the structure and dynamics of the community.

In starting communities of practice to enhance knowledge sharing, it is important to look for *quality* and not *quantity*. The number of participants, like the number of messages or sharing interventions, should not be the indicator for measuring the success of the knowledge sharing process. Rather it should be the quality of knowledge exchanged in the community. "If your strategy is to go for quantity, you often sacrifice quality. If you are driving for as much as possible, you will usually use motivational elements (such as incentives) that will get some people to contribute things for the sake of contributing and not for the sake of potential value" (Leistner, 2010, p. 105). The American Productivity and Quality Center (APQC) analyzed in 2009 how many organizations sustain communities of practice and how those communities create a culture for enhancing knowledge sharing (O'Dell & Hubert, 2011). We present in the next two paragraphs some data from their study on two major companies: ConocoPhillips and Fluor.

ConocoPhillips. This global, integrated energy company is the third-largest oil and gas company in the United States. "Knowledge sharing methods were adapted to promote functional excellence and leverage knowledge across the organization. Knowledge sharing sponsorship is now organization-wide and supported by all business streams" (O'Dell & Hubert, 2011, p. 163). In 2004, top management designed a knowledge strategy to enhance excellence and create a formal framework of such communities as online networks of employees, with a clear agenda and financial support. Today there are more than 120 networks. Access to their portals is free for all employees of the company. To run these networks, the company created a team of knowledge leaders and identified the most significant domains of knowledge sharing for the whole company. Best practices are shared as success stories, which are structured according to a template and validated by the leaders before being uploaded. The strategy of knowledge sharing implemented through these knowledge networks contributed significantly to the value creation of the company by stimulating innovations. The key concept of that success is *trust,* and the policy of FAST: **F**ind the knowledge you need, **A**sk your colleagues about your needs by using the forum, **S**hare your expertise, and **T**rust your colleagues in the community. It is worth mentioning that knowledge leaders are part of the strategic group of the company, and they contribute to strategic decisions. Also, the knowledge sharing strategy includes a reward system for people actively involved in the process of knowledge sharing and leveraging.

Fluor. Fluor Corporation is a global, publicly-traded engineering, construction, and project management organization. The company implemented all generic knowledge strategies with the aim of promoting a global mindset for all its employees. "Leveraging the collective intellectual capital of all employees to support strategic business direction was a key objective. Communities were designed to provide optimal solutions by promoting knowledge across geographic and business-line boundaries" (O'Dell & Hubert, 2011, p. 190). The company designed communities where senior experts share their knowledge with younger colleagues, contributing to the acceleration of organizational learning. Knowledge leaders come up with new projects and ask members of those communities to form project teams based on their competence and to work together to find solutions. Knowledge sharing and knowledge integration are complementary phenomena that lead to ad hoc collective intelligence structures. The climate of trust and intergenerational learning accelerates the knowledge exploitation and knowledge exploration processes. Today, the company has 46 well-defined communities of practice, with more than 24,000 participants and 3,500 subject matter experts. It is an impressive strategic design for enhancing knowledge sharing such that each employee gets the benefits of any knowledge community of practice. These communities integrate the strategies of knowledge sharing and knowledge exploration through their knowledge leaders. "Leaders inspire community members to combine experience and innovation thinking to create new knowledge, and they encourage the community to work smarter through collaboration. Finally, leaders connect the community with strategic direction and drive for business results" (O'Dell & Hubert, 2011, p. 187).

5.5 The Strategy of Knowledge Exploration

5.5.1 Knowledge Creation

The *unknown-unknowns* in a company are hard to identify, but we can imagine the complex and chaotic future with so many unknowns and our present knowledge state unprepared to deal with such an incommensurable absence of knowledge. For people who enjoy living and working in the deterministic zone of *known-knowns*, it is a difficult mental exercise to enter the zone of *unknown-unknowns* and to imagine problems and possible solutions. Knowledge exploration is designed to help managers create conditions for generating knowledge along the main trends in science, technology, economics, business, and consumer behavior. "The essence of exploration is experimentation with new alternatives. Its returns are uncertain, distant, and often negative" (March, 1991, p. 85). In this perspective, knowledge may already exist in the organization but in different structures and combinations. Exploring new alternatives of knowledge structuring by using *lateral thinking* (De Bono, 1970), managers may find new solutions to their problems or stimulate incremental innovation. "Lateral thinking is concerned with the generation of new ideas. There is a curious notion that new ideas have to do with technical invention. This is a very minor aspect of the matter. New ideas are the stuff of change and progress in every field from science to art, from politics to personal happiness" (De Bono, 1970, p. 11).

The strategy of *knowledge exploration* also refers to the process of *knowledge creation* at the individual, team, and organizational levels.

"Similar to scientific knowledge creation it is the experience of new phenomena and problems which let knowledge creation emerge. Organizations
learn as they adapt their 'theory of action' to their changing (internal and
external) environments" (Seirafi, 2013, p. 75). In the philosophy of knowledge management, knowledge creation results from processing information, which represents processed data. It is a hierarchical process embedded
in the Data–Information–Knowledge–Wisdom (DIKW) framework (Davenport
& Prusak, 2000; Jashapara, 2011; Liew, 2013; Rowley, 2007). The DIKW
framework is built on linear logic, but in real life, the data–information–knowledge–wisdom dynamics are nonlinear, such that nobody can explain the phase
transformation between any of these components. The DIKW framework remains
a model of pyramidal complexity of knowledge processing but not as an explan-
ation of its generation.

Nonaka (1994) conceived a model of *knowledge creation* based on the
tension between tacit knowledge and explicit knowledge in a social context.
This model was further refined by Nonaka and Takeuchi (1995) and Nonaka et
al. (2008). The model comprises four processes: Socialization – tacit knowledge exchanged between individuals in a social context called Ba;
Externalization – the transformation of tacit knowledge into explicit knowledge as an embodied process at the individual level; Combination – the
exchange of explicit knowledge in a social context; Internalization – the
transformation of explicit knowledge into tacit knowledge as an embodied
process at the individual level. These four processes run in a cycle called
SECI, generating knowledge at each sequence. The SECI cycle can be
expanded at the team and organizational levels, contributing to organizational
knowledge creation. "Thus, organizational creation can be viewed as an
upward spiral process, starting at the individual level moving up to the
collective (group) level, and then to the organizational level, sometimes
reaching out to the inter-organizational level" (Nonaka, 1994, p. 20).

In epistemology, the fundamental issue is to demonstrate the objectivity of
knowledge. "Thus, a cognitive agent possesses knowledge if it can be rationally
shown that its beliefs are true. The main epistemological question then is, how
knowledge is justified, i.e. how the separation between mere beliefs and knowledge is accomplished" (Seirafi, 2013, p. 107). In knowledge management, the
semantic domain of *knowledge* has been enlarged such that it contains both
objective and subjective aspects. In this situation, Nonaka (1994, p. 15) considers knowledge a result of the "human process of justifying personal beliefs as
part of an aspiration for the truth." Thus, the Nonakian philosophy of knowledge
creation contains two phases. In the first phase, knowledge is generated and
amplified in the SECI cycle, and in the second phase, knowledge is justified as a

true belief through social interaction in a certain Ba. In this view, justification is realized in direct confrontation with the organizational culture.

Bratianu (2015a) described knowledge dynamics as a continuous interaction between the rational, emotional, and spiritual fields. So, knowledge creation can result from the transformation of one form of knowledge into another or from the restructuring of rational knowledge because of an exchange of knowledge between different cognitive agents. As emphasized by Kolb (2015, p. 43), "To learn is not the special province of a single specialized realm of human functioning such as cognition or perception. It involves the integrated functioning of the total organism – thinking, feeling, perceiving, and behaving." All the data and information we receive through our sensory system are transformed into emotional knowledge in our body and cognitive unconscious, and then through the interaction of knowledge fields, emotional knowledge is transformed into new rational knowledge and integrated into the cognitive structure of the individual. Through social interaction, individual knowledge is amplified and transformed into organizational knowledge. Thus, knowledge creation originates in our practice as new data. Those data are processed by the sensory system into emotional information and emotional knowledge by the cognitive unconscious. Through the interaction of the rational and emotional fields, emotional knowledge is transformed into rational knowledge as a result of reflection. Finally, in time, both emotional and rational knowledge contribute to generating spiritual knowledge (Damasio, 1999, 2003, 2012; Fauconnier & Turner, 2002; Friedenberg & Silverman, 2016; LeDoux, 1999; Robinson et al., 2013).

5.5.2 Knowledge Exploration and Innovation

Innovation is the key process sustaining a competitive advantage, not only for firms but for countries as well (Khazanchi et al., 2007; Newell et al., 2009; Tellis et al., 2009). As Richard Florida (2004, 2007) showed in his famous studies based on impressive statistical work, innovation supported by creative people becomes a global driving force that changes not only economies but also social structures. "I call the age we are entering the creative age because the key factor propelling us forward is the rise of creativity as the prime mover of our economy. Not just technology or information, but human creativity" (Florida, 2007, p. 26).

Innovation is a complex process that integrates knowledge creation and aims at embedding the new knowledge and ideas into new products and services to satisfy the changing needs of consumers. Traditionally, innovation was conceived as a rational and linear process composed of knowledge creation, knowledge diffusion, knowledge implementation, and knowledge usage (Newell et al., 2009). That model presented in a simple way the phases of product innovation in the industrial era. Today, many researchers have shown that innovation is not based on rational knowledge alone, but it includes irrational knowledge which reflects the intuition and emotional knowledge (Ariely, 2011; Nussbaum, 2001; Sutherland, 2013). Innovation is a complex, nonlinear, and interactive process with many unknowns and unexpected outcomes. "Innovation is a dynamic design and decision process that is by nature both iterative and recursive and mediated by a range of cognitive, social and organizational factors" (Newell et al., 2009, 195).

Innovation requires solid personal motivation and good support from the company's management and organizational culture. Ideas are generated by individuals, but their implementation needs resources, and those resources are allocated by managers. Moreover, innovation involves a series of risks, which must be assumed by managers and supported by the organizational culture. Developing innovation in knowledge-intensive business services (KIBS) switches the focus from product to service innovation and from the traditional R&D department to the whole organization and its consumer base.

Because of the increasing role of networks and networking processes, innovation today becomes an open-ended process with contributions from many different actors, including consumers. Open innovation is supported by a new managerial philosophy and new software applications (Chesbrough, 2004). Open innovation extends knowledge creation toward knowledge co-creation, a much more complex process with external collaborators and a large spectrum of business interests. It contributes to the development of the new phenomenon of *crowdsourcing* (Brabham, 2013; Downes & Nunes, 2014). "The interplay between crowd and organization is crucial for crowdsourcing because it ensures a mutually beneficial outcome that probably could not have existed without the creative efforts of both parties" (Brabham, 2013, p. 4). That requires a different mindset from managers and a deeper understanding of knowledge risks and intellectual property.

6 Emergent Knowledge Strategies

6.1 The Strategy of Organizational Learning

When the future is emerging without any deterministic algorithm, *deliberate knowledge strategies* cannot answer new business challenges. They have to be replaced with *emergent knowledge strategies*. These strategies are based on the metaphor of the stationary observer and moving time; they belong to the *learning school,* as explained by Mintzberg et al. (1998), and they fit the *processual* category of strategies defined by Whittington (2001).

The expression *emergent knowledge strategy* looks like an oxymoron since a *strategy* implies thinking ahead of time while *emergent* refers to an evolving process as a reaction to an external force or event. The semantic conflict between these terms defines the essence of the concept because an emergent strategy represents a reaction to unpredictable changes in the external business environment, but it is supported by the strategic thinking in a firm's vision and mission framework. Mintzberg & Waters (1985) consider that a *deliberate strategy* can be conceived as *a pattern in a stream of decisions*, while an *emergent strategy* can be understood as *a pattern in a stream of behaviors*. In the first case, the emphasis is on strategic thinking. In the second case, the emphasis is on actions with long-term consequences. These actions represent a reaction to some unpredictable changes in the external environment, but they are supported by a strategic mindset and lead to a learning process. "In our view, the fundamental difference between deliberate and emergent strategy is that whereas the former focuses on direction and control—getting desired things done—the latter opens up this notion of *strategic learning*" (Mintzberg & Waters, 1985, p. 270).

Organizational learning is a construct based on the metaphor of an organism capable of learning to adapt to its environment (Maier et al., 2003). Organizational learning is a learning process performed by multiple intelligent agents in a social context. It is an interactive process generated in a social system like a team, department, or organization. Through organizational learning, "whole organizations or their components adapt to changing environments by generating and selectively adopting organizational routines" (Argyris, 1999, p. 8). When organizational learning extends to the level of the whole organization, becoming a systems process, the organization is transformed into a *learning organization* (Argote, 2013; Senge, 1999). In such an organization, learning becomes a continuous process of integrating experiential knowledge with reflection and creating knowledge for the emerging future. The learning organization can get out of the survival state by transforming *adaptive learning* into *generative learning* (Senge, 1999). Adaptive learning is based on imitating the best companies and transferring best practices. An emergent strategy is useful when a company is in an economic survival phase and needs knowledge to craft strategies used by a successful company. However, the transfer of best practices has limited results since the organizational context is different. When adaptive learning is focused on the internal business environment, then *kaizen* or continuous improvement can sustain emergent strategies. It is the Japanese approach that prefers incremental learning based on the PDCA cycle, as we explained in a previous section (Nonaka & Takeuchi, 1995; Rother, 2010).

Generative learning is based on *systems thinking* and the new paradigm of *learning to learn* (Jackson, 2019; Senge, 1999). It is an entropic process oriented toward the future and a nonlinear process that allows rational and irrational thinking to interact and create new value. "Generative learning cannot be sustained in an organization if people's thinking is dominated by short-term events. If we focus on events, the best we can do is predict before it happens so that we can react optimally. But we cannot learn to create" (Senge, 1999, p. 22). Generative learning is capable of creating the critical knowledge needed when the future comes with unexpected events and a significant absence of knowledge. The learning organization might be interpreted as an ideal organization or as a strange attractor, since real organizations always have inertial forces that slow down change processes and any attempt to integrate timely experiential learning with reflection and logical thinking. It is important when discussing learning organizations to avoid the binary logic of being or not being a learning organization since learning is always an ongoing process. Thus, it would be preferable to discuss the level of organizational learning and its contribution to the development of a learning organization. Generative learning is a self-sustainable process if there is an adequate organizational culture. It is a bridge over the dynamic gap between the known and the unknown (Rumelt, 2012). In such a new culture, errors, failures, and breakdowns are accepted and considered opportunities for learning – not reasons for punishing the workers. Experts analyze these work discontinuities and try to identify the factors which lead to bad results. Usually, these factors have a human, technological, managerial, or mixed origin. Learning their origin helps to identify practical ways to mitigate their influence. Spender and Strong (2014, p. 137) show that "doing things that matter involves risking failure. Many organizations these days speak of 'smart failure' and the importance of taking risks to explore new opportunities." Thus, designing emergent strategies requires accepting risks and smart failures to exploit the firm's opportunity space.

From the perspective of systems thinking, Argyris (1999) considers learning organizations to have *double-loop learning*. Single-loop learning is useful for corrections when there are repetitive actions or programmable routines. It is the known feedback loop of cybernetic systems, which acts upon the input variables. Double-loop learning is necessary for activities that are not programmable and when the system is working in a changeable environment. Such a learning loop creates the possibility of changing the governing variables, a profound change that cannot be done in organizations that have only single-loop learning. At a different scale and switching from the individual to the organizational level, double-loop learning is similar to the Learning II mode, or deuteron-learning, defined by Bateson (2000).

6.2 The Strategy of Scenario Design

When we discussed future perception, we emphasized that the future should be understood as a series of possible events and not as an extension of the present time. Furthermore, we may imagine several possible futures, not just one. Thus, we may create scenarios for those possible futures by considering the key uncertainties we have in the present (De Ruijter & Alkema, 2014; Syrett & Devine, 2012). "Scenarios are images of the future constructed by combining possible developments in different ways. In this way, imaginary situations are created which you can explore" (De Ruijter & Alkema, 2014, p. 56).

Designing possible scenarios for the future of an organization is not a goal in itself, nor should it be because there is an infinite number of such possible scenarios. When the external business environment becomes turbulent, and we want to know what will happen with the firm in an uncertain future, scenario thinking is just a *conceptual instrument* for stretching our imagination and creating some possible evolutions of the firm, each of them with possible opportunities and associated risks. That helps managers to make better decisions under the stress of uncertainty and absence of knowledge. The key issue in scenario design is not finding the best scenario that will happen but providing a series of probable scenarios that might happen. The emergent future might not fit any one of those scenarios, but it might aggregate many of the aspects already defined with them. Thus, the emergent strategy builds conceptual support for the decision-making process when the future brings unexpected events.

Scenario thinking was pioneering in Shell's planning department in 1971, when Ted Newland led a new group of people who imagined possible oil price evolutions in a given geopolitical framework. When the oil crisis came in 1973, Shell managers were mentally prepared for designing emergent strategies that helped the company overcome that unexpected oil crisis. That made the difference between Shell's reaction and the responses of competitors who were not prepared for the events created by OPEC. From that time on, scenario thinking became an integral part of Shell's strategy design (De Geus, 2002).

> They realized that for an organization, it is not as important to have a clear view of *what will happen,* as on *the different things which could happen.* This was the turning point from a single view of the future, or a single prediction, to multiple views of the future or predictions, based on the same model of structures and influencing factors. (De Ruijter & Alkema, 2014, p. 57).

The purpose of *scenario thinking* is not *to predict* the future, but *to explore* it based on the trends identified at the present time and on the key uncertainties considered in that phase. MacKay & McKiernan (2018, p. 39) define scenario thinking as "a cognitive process concerned with imagining how the future unfolds in multiple ways through the analysis and judgment of the effects of the actions and reactions of shaping forces." Scenario thinking is transposed then in descriptive narratives or stories to create a spectrum of possible futures for the company. Then, for each of these possible futures, there are some actions associated with their implementation, if necessary. The strategy of designing scenarios integrates the three stages of thinking, developing stories, and actions for implementation. Companies prepared with such strategies can react faster and smarter than their competitors when the future emerges with unexpected events.

One practical issue of scenario design is determining the *time horizon*. This is important when a business domain must select the corporate strategies to integrate the knowledge strategies. In practice, the time horizon for public institutions is about four years, since governmental policies are usually elaborated for that time period. For projects with large strategic objectives like constructing power plants, artificial lakes, or islands, the time horizon may be extended to ten or fifteen years, or even more.

Another issue is to determine the key uncertainties for which a company develops scenarios. First, these uncertainties are identified. Second, each uncertainty is analyzed with respect to its possible influence on the performance of the company. Finally, those uncertainties that might have a more powerful impact on the company's future are selected as starting points for scenario thinking. Scenario design is not linear, and it follows no predetermined algorithm. It is a nonlinear process with many iterations and changes as a result of combining different influencing factors. Intuition and deduction are used alternately to obtain a certain consistency in the overall design. Because subjective thinking dominates, the validity of a scenario design cannot be tested. However, it should be analyzed for its plausibility and consistency with the initial hypotheses. Logical thinking and even mathematical modeling are not ignored in scenario design, but they are used when the basic framework that incorporates human subjectivity is well defined.

In conclusion, a scenario is an aggregation of possible future developments which lead to a final state for that future. The real future might not follow that scenario exactly, but it could be very close to it. Thus, the company is prepared for a fast and adequate reaction to that emergent future. Scenario thinking introduces a new way to conceive the future and to design strategies for that possible future. Practice has shown that for a company that uses the strategy of scenario design, developing scenario thinking is more important than the scenarios themselves. Emergent strategies are based on strategic thinking and not on predetermined plans which no longer fit the changes produced in the external business environment.

7 Integrated Knowledge Strategies

Knowledge strategies represent our answer to the continuously increasing ratio between intangible and tangible resources in companies, especially in knowledge-intensive organizations, and to the unexpected dynamics of the future. Knowledge strategies integrate into corporate strategies and align with the firm's vision. As Barnes and Milton (2015, p. 24) underscore, "If we are going to do our jobs properly as knowledge managers, we need to start from organizational strategy, organizational needs, and organizational outcomes at all levels. It is vital that KM efforts are linked to organizational outcomes because outcomes are what is important." Knowledge strategies are implemented at the level of the whole organization, and all employees should be aware of them because of the organizational changes that will follow.

At the same time, knowledge strategies are integrated entities because they combine deliberate and emergent knowledge strategies. We have presented generic strategies and emergent strategies separately for an academic purpose, but in practice, each strategy comprises a *deliberate* or proactive component and an *emergent* or reactive component, which interact in time and space. That interaction is driven by the implementation process. In a deliberate strategy, we start from what we know best – the initial phase – while in the emergent strategy, we start with what we don't know or with the absence of knowledge. That is an interesting interaction between known and unknown, between certainty and uncertainty. Thus, integrated knowledge strategies are based on the dynamics of *known-unknowns*, and that is the main difference between them and corporate strategies.

Nonaka and Zhu (2012, p. 34) remark that "Whereas in the 'West' uncertainty is usually considered a source of grief to be contained, in Confucianism uncertainty is a desirable quality." That remark can be elaborated by considering the different attitudes toward fuzziness in the West and the East. In the West, people strive for well-defined ideas and precise language expressions, but in the East, people prefer fuzzy ideas and language expressions. These different approaches generate differences in ways of thinking and in designing strategies. As a consequence, in the context of American management, knowledge strategies focus more on the deliberate components, while in the Chinese and Japanese contexts, knowledge strategies focus more on the emergent aspects. "To people involved in the emergence process, strategic outcome is a combination of intended and unintended consequences, of managerial actions and environmental factors"

(Nonaka & Zhu, 2012, p. 128). This idea is closely related to the fact that for the Chinese and Japanese managers, knowledge is not as much a representation of the external world as it is a capacity to act, to perform. "The reason is plain and simple: pragmatism engages people to act upon what works, and the real world appears to reward what works and what doesn't" (Nonaka & Zhu, 2012, p. 25).

A knowledge strategy also manifests its integration force in the rational, emotional, and spiritual knowledge fields. These fields interact continuously, generating a synergy effect (Bratianu & Bejinaru, 2019). Rational knowledge is used predominantly in the design of deliberate strategies, especially the exploitation and acquisition strategies. Emotional and spiritual knowledge becomes important for implementing knowledge sharing and knowledge exploration strategies and for learning emergent strategies. Implementing knowledge strategies leads to organizational change that depends on the way emotional and spiritual knowledge is used by managers. Visionary leaders and organizational culture, as nonlinear organizational integrators, play an important role in the process of integrating knowledge fields into knowledge strategies, and knowledge strategies into corporate strategies (Bratianu, 2013; Mintzberg et al., 1998; Nonaka & Takeuchi, 1995; Nonaka & Zhu, 2012). Visionary leaders define the goals and direction of the knowledge strategy, which is aligned with the corporate strategy, and the organizational culture supports the successful implementation of the strategy. "When such alignment between the knowledge management strategy and the business strategy is clearly established, the knowledge management system is moving in a direction that holds promise for long-lasting competitive advantage" (Snyman & Kruger, 2004, p. 5).

Nonaka and Zhu (2012, p. 1650) illustrate the integration effect of managerial practice with Confucian wisdom: "From this we construct a triple-strategy bottom line (WSR): *wuli*, the material-technical, *shili*, the cognitive-mental, and *renli*, the social-relational. Pragmatic strategies based on WSR generate value efficiently, creatively and legitimately by getting fundamentals right, envisioning a valued future and realizing common goodness." This perspective is important for knowledge strategies because they operate with intangible resources, but their implementation is conditioned by the objective reality of the company, with its material infrastructure, and the social context. The focus of knowledge strategies is not on maximizing the profit of shareholders but on creating the conditions for achieving a competitive advantage in the market. The power of knowledge strategies resides in their goal of reducing the absence of knowledge and of decreasing the level of uncertainty. Their outcomes directly influence the design of corporate strategies, which cannot be conceived without adequate knowledge.

Finally, knowledge strategies result from the intersection of strategic thinking and knowledge management, or from the integration of the corporate vision and mission with organizational knowledge. Knowledge strategies are used in the domain of knowledge management, and they are integrated into corporate strategies.

References

Agarwal, N. K. & Islam, M. A. 2015. Knowledge retention and transfer: How libraries manage employees leaving and joining. *VINE Journal of Information and Knowledge Management Systems*, 45(2), 150–71.

Albrecht, K. 2003. *The power of minds at work: Organizational intelligence in action*. New York: American Management Association.

Andrews, K. R. 1971. *The concept of corporate strategy*. Homewood, IL: Irwin.

Andriessen, D. 2004. *Making sense of intellectual capital: Designing a method for the valuation of intangibles*. Amsterdam: Elsevier.

Andriopoulos, C. & Lewis, M. 2009. Exploitation-exploration tensions and organizational ambidexterity: Managing paradoxes of innovation. *Organization Science*, 20(4), 696–717.

Ansoff, I. 1965. *Corporate strategy*. Harmondsworth: Penguin.

Aoki, M. 1996. The Japanese firm as a system of attributes: A survey and research agenda. In Aoki, M. & Dore, R. (eds.). *The Japanese firm: Sources of competitive strength*. Oxford: Oxford University Press, pp. 11–41.

Argote, L. 2013. *Organizational learning: Creating, retaining and transferring knowledge*. 2nd ed. New York: Springer.

Argote, L. & Miron-Spektor, E. 2011. Organizational learning: From experience to knowledge. *Organization Science*, 22(5), 1123–37.

Argyris, C. 1999. *On organizational learning*. 2nd ed. Oxford: Blackwell.

Ariely, D. 2011. *The upside of irrationality: The unexpected benefits of defying logic at work and at home*. London: HarperCollins.

Atkins, P. 2010. *The laws of thermodynamics: A very short introduction*. Oxford: Oxford University Press.

Balconi, M. 2002. Tacitness, codification of technological knowledge, and the organization of industry. *Research Policy*, 31(3), 357–79.

Barnard, C. I. 1938. *The functions of the executive*. Cambridge, MA: Harvard University Press.

Barnard, C. I. 1968. *The functions of the executive*. Introduction by Kenneth R. Andrews. 30th anniversary ed. Cambridge, MA: Harvard University Press.

Barnes, S. & Milton, N. 2015. *Designing a successful KM strategy: A guide for the knowledge management professional*. Medford, NJ: Information Today.

Barney, J. B. 1991. Firm resources and sustained competitive advantage. *Journal of Management*, 17(1), 99–120.

Barney, J. B. & Clark, D. N. 2007. *Resource-based theory: Creating and sustaining competitive advantage*. Oxford: Oxford University Press.

Barney, J. B. & Hesterly, W. S. 2012. *Strategic management and competitive advantage: Concepts and cases.* New York: Pearson.

Bateson, G. 2000. *Steps to an ecology of mind.* Chicago: University of Chicago Press.

Bereiter, C. 2002. *Education and mind in the knowledge age.* London: Routledge.

Bernstein, P. L. 1998. *Against the gods: The remarkable story of risk.* New York: John Wiley & Sons.

Bolisani, E. & Bratianu, C. 2018. *Emergent knowledge strategies: Strategic thinking in knowledge management.* Cham: Springer International Publishing.

Bolisani, E. & Oltramari, A. 2012. Knowledge as a measurable object in business contexts: A stock-and-flow approach. *Knowledge Management Research & Practice*, 10(3), 275–86.

Bolisani, E., Paiola, M. & Scarso, E. 2013. Knowledge protection in knowledge-intensive business services. *Journal of Intellectual Capital*, 14 (2), 192–211.

Boroditsky, L. 2000. Metaphoric structuring: Understanding time through spatial metaphors. *Cognition*, 75, 1–28.

Bose, P. 2004. *Alexander the Great: Art of strategy. Lessons from the great empire builder.* London: Profile Books.

Brabham, D. C. 2013. *Crowdsourcing.* Cambridge, MA: MIT Press.

Branson, R. 2009. *Business stripped bare: Adventures of a global entrepreneur.* London: Virgin Books.

Bratianu, C. 2009. The frontier of linearity in the intellectual capital metaphor. *The Electronic Journal of Knowledge Management*, 7(4), 415–24.

Bratianu, C. 2011. Changing paradigm for knowledge metaphors from dynamics to thermodynamics. *Systems Research and Behavioral Science*, 28(2), 160–9.

Bratianu, C. 2013. Nonlinear integrators of the organizational intellectual capital. In Fathi, M. (ed.). *Integration of practice-oriented knowledge technology: Trends and perspectives.* Heidelberg: Springer, pp. 3–16.

Bratianu, C. 2015a. *Organizational knowledge dynamics: Managing knowledge creation, acquisition, sharing, and transformation.* Hershey, PA: IGI Global.

Bratianu, C. 2015b. Developing strategic thinking in business education. *Management Dynamics in the Knowledge Economy*, 3(3), 409–29.

Bratianu, C. 2016. Knowledge dynamics. *Management Dynamics in the Knowledge Economy*, 4(3), 323–37.

Bratianu, C. 2018a. Intellectual capital research and practice: 7 myths and one golden rule. *Management & Marketing: Challenges for the Knowledge Society*, 13(2), 859–79.

Bratianu, C. 2018b. A holistic approach to knowledge risk. *Management Dynamics in the Knowledge Economy*, 6(4), 593–607.

Bratianu, C. 2019. Exploring knowledge entropy in organizations. *Management Dynamics in the Knowledge Economy*, 7(3), 353–66.

Bratianu, C. & Bejinaru, R. 2019. The theory of knowledge fields: A thermodynamic approach. *Systems*, 7(2), 20.

Bratianu, C. & Leon, R. D. 2015. Strategies to enhance intergenerational learning and reducing knowledge loss. *VINE Journal of Information and Knowledge Management Systems*, 45(4), 551–67.

Bratianu, C. & Vatamanescu, E. M. 2018. The entropic knowledge dynamics as a driving force of the decision-making process. *The Electronic Journal of Knowledge Management*, 16(1), 1–12.

Bratianu, C., Agapie, A. & Orzea, I. 2011. Modeling organizational knowledge dynamics: Using analytic hierarchy process (AHP). *The Electronic Journal of Knowledge Management*, 9(3), 236–47.

Braunerhjelm, P., Acs, Z. J., Audredtsch, D. & Carlsson, B. 2010. The missing link: Knowledge diffusion and entrepreneurship in endogenous growth. *Small Business Economics*, 34(2), 105–25.

Brown, J. S. & Duguid, P. 1998. Organizing knowledge. *California Management Review*, 40(3), 90–111.

Buzan, T. & Buzan, B. 1993. *The mind map book: How to use radiant thinking to maximize your brain's untapped potential*. New York: Plume.

Casasanto, D. & Jasmin, K. 2012. The hands of time: Temporal gestures in English speakers. *Cognitive Linguistics*, 23(4), 643–74.

Castelfranchi, C. & Falcone, R. 2010. *Trust theory: A socio-cognitive and computational model*. Chichester, UK: John Wiley & Sons.

Chaldize, V. 2000. *Entropy demystified: Potential order, life and money*. Portland, OR: Universal Publishing.

Chan I. & Chao, C. K. 2008. Knowledge management in small and medium-sized enterprises. *Communications of the ACM*, 51(4), 83–8.

Chandler, A. D. 1962. *Strategy and structure: Chapters in the history of the American industrial enterprise*. Cambridge, MA: MIT Press.

Chaston, I. & Mangles, T. 2000. Business networks: Assisting knowledge management and competence acquisition within UK manufacturing firms. *Journal of Small Business and Enterprise Development*, 7(2), 160–70.

Chesbrough, H. 2004. Managing open innovation. *Research Technology Management*, 47, 23–6.

Clark, R. E., Feldon, D. F., van Merrieboer, J. J. G., Yates, K. A. & Early, S. 2008. Cognitive task analysis. In Spector, J. M. & Driscall, M. D. (eds.).

Handbook of research on educational communications and technology. 3rd edition. New York: Taylor & Francis, pp. 578–93.

Clausewitz, C. von. 1989. *On war.* Princeton, NJ: Princeton University Press.

Coase, R. H. 1937. The nature of the firm. *Economica,* 4(16), 386–405.

Cohen, W. M. & Levinthal, D. A. 1990. Absorptive capacity: A new perspective on learning and innovation. *Administrative Science Quarterly,* 35(1), 128–52.

Cyr, S. & Choo, C. W. 2010. The individual and social dynamics of knowledge sharing: An exploratory study. *The Journal of Documentation,* 66(6), 824–46.

Dalkir, K. 2005. *Knowledge management in theory and practice.* New York: Elsevier.

Damasio, A. R. 1999. *The feelings of what happens: Body and emotion in making of conscious.* New York: Harcourt.

Damasio, A. R. 2003. *Looking for Spinoza: Joy, sorrow, and the feeling brain.* New York: Harcourt.

Damasio, A. R. 2012. *Self comes to mind: Constructing the conscious brain.* New York: Vintage Book.

Davenport, T. H. & Prusak, L. 2000. *Working knowledge: How organizations manage what they know.* Boston, MA: Harvard Business School Press.

De Bono, E. 1970. *Lateral thinking: Creativity step by step.* New York: Harper & Row.

De Geus, A. 2002. *The living company: Growth and longevity in business.* London: Nicholas Brealey.

DeLong, D. W. 2004. *Lost knowledge: Confronting the threat of an aging workforce.* Oxford: Oxford University Press.

De Ruijter, P. & Alkema, H. 2014. *Scenario based strategy: Navigate the future.* Farnham: Gower Publishing.

Dess, G. G., McNamara, G., Eisner, A. B. & Lee, S. H. 2018. *Strategic management.* New York: McGraw-Hill Irwin.

Doloreaux, D., Freel, M. S. & Shearmur, R. G. (eds.). 2010. *Knowledge-intensive business services: Geography and innovation.* Aldershot, UK: Ashgate Publishing.

Donate, M. J. & Canales, J. I. 2012. A new approach to the concept of knowledge strategy. *Journal of Knowledge Management,* 16(1), 22–44.

Downes, L. & Nunes, P. 2014. *Big bang disruption: Business survival in the age of constant innovation.* London: Portfolio Penguin.

Doz, Y. & Kosonen, M. 2008. *Fast strategy: How strategic agility will help you stay ahead of the game.* London: Wharton School Publishing.

Drucker, P. F. 1993. *Management: Tasks, responsibilities, practices.* New York: Harper Business.

Drucker, P. F. 2001. *Management challenges for the 21ˢᵗ century.* New York: Harper Business.

Dumay, J. 2016. A critical reflection on the future of intellectual capital: From reporting to disclosure. *Journal of Intellectual Capital,* 17(1), 168–84.

Durst, S. 2019. How far have we come with the study of knowledge risks? *VINE Journal of Information and Knowledge Management Systems,* 49(1), 21–34.

Durst, S. & Edvardson, I. R. 2012. Knowledge management in SMEs: A literature review. *Journal of Knowledge Management,* 16(6), 879–903.

Durst, S. & Zieba, M. 2017. Knowledge risks – a taxonomy. *International Journal of Business Environment,* 9(1), 51–63.

Edvinsson, L. 2002. *Corporate longitude: What you need to know to navigate the knowledge economy.* London: Prentice Hall.

Eucker, T. R. 2007. Understanding the impact of tacit knowledge loss. *KM Review,* 10(2), 10–13.

Fauconnier, G. & Turner, M. 2002. *The way we think: Conceptual blending and the mind's hidden complexities.* New York: Basic Books.

Florida, R. 2004. *The rise of the creative class: And how it's transforming work, leisure, community and everyday life.* New York: Basic Books.

Florida, R. 2007. *The flight of the creative class: The new global competition for talent.* New York: HarperCollins Publishers.

Friedenberg, J. & Silverman, G. 2016. *Cognitive science: An introduction to the study of mind.* 3rd edition. London: SAGE.

Frith, C. 2007. *Making up the mind: How the brain creates our mental world.* Malden, MA: Blackwell Publishing.

Georgescu-Roegen, N. 1999. *The entropy law and the economic process.* Cambridge, MA: Harvard University Press.

Gerstner, Jr., L. 2003. *Who says elephants can't dance? How I turned around IBM.* London: Harper Collins Publishers.

Gladwell, M. 2008. *Outliers: The story of success.* London: Penguin Books.

Gleick, J. 2008. *Chaos: Making a new science.* New York: Penguin Books.

Grant, R. 1991. The resource-based theory of competitive advantage: Implications for strategy formulation. *California Management Review,* 33 (3), 114–35.

Grant, R. 1996. Towards a knowledge-based theory of the firm. *Strategic Management Journal,* 17, Special Issue, 109–22.

Grant, R. 1997. The knowledge-based view of the firm: Implications for management practice. *Long Range Planning,* 30(3), 450–54.

Güth, W. & Kliemt, H. 2017. How to cope with (new) uncertainties: A bounded rationality approach. *Homo Oecon,* 34, 343–59.

Guthrie, J., Ricceri, F. & Dumay, J. 2012. Reflections and projections: A decade of intellectual capital accounting research. *The British Accounting Review*, 44 (2), 68–82.

Haig. M. 2003. *Brand failures: The truth about the 100 biggest branding mistakes of all time*. London: Kogan Page.

Hamel, G. & Prahalad, C. K. 1994. *Competing for the future*. Boston, MA: Harvard Business School.

Henderson, B. D. 1989. The origin of strategy. *Harvard Business Review*, November–December, 139–43.

Hill, C. W. L. & Jones, G. R. 1998. *Strategic management: An integrated approach*. 4th edition. Boston, MA: Houghton Mifflin Company.

Hill, D. 2008. *Emotionomics: Leveraging emotions for business success*. Revised edition. London: Kogan Page.

Hipel, E. von. 1994. 'Sticky information' and the locus of problem solving: Implications for innovations. *Management Science*, 40(4), 429–39.

Hislop, D. 2005. *Knowledge management in organizations: A critical introduction*. Oxford: Oxford University Press.

Hoe, S. L. & McShane, S. 2010. Structural and informal knowledge acquisition and dissemination in organizational learning: An exploratory analysis. *The Learning Organization*, 17(4), 364–86.

Hoshi, T. 1996. The economic role of corporate grouping and the main bank system. In Aoki, M. & Dore, R. (eds.). *The Japanese firm: Sources of competitive strength*. Oxford: Oxford University Press, pp. 285–310.

Ichijo, K. 2007. The strategic management of knowledge. In Ichijo, K. & Nonaka, I. (eds.). *Knowledge creation and management: New challenges for managers*. Oxford: Oxford University Press, pp. 83–96.

Isaacson, W. 2011. *Steve Jobs*. London: Little, Brown.

Isaacson, W. 2014. *The innovators: How a group of hackers, geniuses, and geeks created the digital revolution*. New York: Simon & Schuster.

Jackson, M. C. 2019. *Critical systems thinking and the management of complexity*. New York: John Wiley & Sons.

Jashapara, A. 2011. *Knowledge management: An integrated approach*. 2nd edition. London: Financial Times/Prentice Hall.

Johnson, G., Whittington, R., Scholes, K., Angwin, D. & Regner, P. 2017. *Exploring corporate strategy: Text & cases*. 11th edition. London: Prentice Hall.

Kahneman, D. 2011. *Thinking, fast and slow*. New York: Farrar, Straus and Giroux.

Kahney, L. 2008. *Inside Steve's brain*. London: Atlantic Books.

Kaufman, S. F. 1994. *The martial artist's book of five rings: The definitive interpretation of Miyamoto Musashi's classic book of strategy.* Boston, MA: Tuttle Publishing.

Khazanchi, S., Lewis, M. W. & Boyer, K. K. 2007. Innovation-supportive culture: The impact of organizational values on process innovation. *Journal of Operations Management*, 25, 871–84.

Kim, S., Suh, E. & Hwang, H. 2003. Building the knowledge map: An industrial case study. *Journal of Knowledge Management*, 7(2), 34–45.

Klein, G. 2003. *The power of intuition: How to use your gut feelings to make better decisions at work.* New York: Currency Doubleday.

Knight, F. H. 2006. *Risk, uncertainty and profit.* New York: Dover Publications.

Kodama, M. 2011. *Knowledge integration dynamics: Developing strategic innovation capability.* Singapore: World Scientific.

Kolb, D. A. 2015. *Experiential learning: Experience as a source of learning and development.* 2nd edition. Upper Saddle River, NJ: Pearson Education.

Kotter, J. P. 1996. *Leading change.* Boston, MA: Harvard Business School Press.

Kotter, J. P. 2008. *A sense of urgency.* Boston, MA: Harvard Business School Press.

Kudryavtsev, D. & Gavrilova, T. 2017. From anarchy to system: A novel classification on visual knowledge codification techniques. *Knowledge and Process Management*, 24(1), 3–13.

Lakoff, G. & Johnson, M. 1980. *Metaphors we live by.* Chicago: The University of Chicago Press.

Lakoff, G. & Johnson, M. 1999. *Philosophy in the flesh: The embodied mind and its challenge to western thought.* New York: Basic Books.

Landry, R., Amara, N. & Doloreaux, D. 2012. Knowledge-exchange strategies between KIBS firms and their clients. *The Service Industries Journal*, 32(2), 291–320.

LeDoux, J. 1999. *The emotional brain: The mysterious underpinnings of emotional life.* London: Phoenix.

Lefter, V., Bratianu, C., Agapie, A., Agoston, S. & Orzea, I. 2011. Intergenerational knowledge transfer in the academic environment of knowledge-based economy. *Amfiteatru Economic Journal*, 13(30), 392–403.

Leistner, F. 2010. *Mastering organizational knowledge flow: How to make knowledge sharing work.* Hoboken, NJ: John Wiley & Sons.

Liao, S. H., Wu, C. C., Hu, D. C. & Tsui, K. A. 2010. Relationships between knowledge acquisition, absorptive capacity and innovation capability: An empirical study on Taiwan's financial and manufacturing industries. *Journal of Information Science*, 36(1), 19–35.

Liebowitz, J. 2005. Linking social network analysis with the analytic hierarchy process for knowledge mapping in organizations. *Journal of Knowledge Management*, 9(1), 76–86.

Liew, A. 2013. DIKIW: Data, information, knowledge, intelligence, wisdom and their interrelationships. *Business Management Dynamics*, 2(10), 49–62.

Lindley, D. V. 2006. *Understanding uncertainty*. Hoboken, NJ: Wiley-Interscience.

MacKay, B. & McKiernan, P. 2018. *Scenario thinking: A historical evolution of strategic foresight*. Cambridge: Cambridge University Press.

Maier, G. W., Prange, C. & Von Rosenstiel, L. 2003. Psychological perspectives of organizational learning. In Dierkes, M., Berthoin Antal, A., Child, J. & Nonaka, I. (eds.). *Handbook of organizational learning & knowledge*. Oxford: Oxford University Press, pp. 14–34.

March, J. G. 1991. Exploration and exploitation in organizational learning. *Organization Science*, 2(1), 71–87.

Martins, E. C. & Meyer, H. W. J. 2012. Organizational and behavioral factors that influence knowledge retention. *Journal of Knowledge Management*, 16 (1), 77–96.

Maxwell, N. 2007. *From knowledge to wisdom: A revolution for science and the humanities*. 2nd edition. London: Pentire Press.

Mayer, R. C., Davis, J. H. & Schoorman, F. D. 1995. An integrative model of organizational trust. *Academy of Management Review*, 20(3), 709–34.

Mellahi, K., Frynas, G.J. & Finlay, P. 2005. *Global strategic management*. Oxford, UK: Oxford University Press.

Milton, N. R. 2007. *Knowledge acquisition in practice: A step-by-step guide*. Berlin: Springer.

Mintzberg, H. 2000. *The rise and fall of strategic planning*. London: Prentice Hall.

Mintzberg, H., Ahlstrand, B. & Lampel, J. 1998. *Strategy safari: The complete guide through the wilds of strategic management*. London: Prentice Hall.

Mintzberg, H. & Waters, J. 1985. Of strategies, deliberate and emergent. *Strategic Management Journal*, 6(3), 257–72.

Morgan, G. 1997. *Images of organization*. London: SAGE Publications.

Morone, J. & Taylor, R. 2004. Knowledge diffusion dynamics and network properties of face-to-face interactions. *Journal of Evolutionary Economics*, 14(3), 327–51.

Murgatroyd, S. 2015. *How to rethink the future: Making use of strategic foresight*. Alberta: The Collaborative Media Group.

Nesheim, T. & Gressgard, L. J. 2014. Knowledge sharing in a complex organization: Antecedents and safety effects. *Safety Science*, 62, 28–36.

Newell, S., Robertson, M., Scarbrough, H. & Swan, J. 2009. *Managing knowledge work and innovation*. 2nd edition. Houndmills, UK: Palgrave Macmillan.

Nickerson, J. A. & Zenger, T. R. 2004. A knowledge-based theory of the firm: The problem-solving perspective. *Organization Science*, 15(6), 617–32.

Nisbett, R. E. 2003. *The geography of thought: How Asians and Westerners think differently . . . and why*. New York: Free Press.

Nissen, M. E. 2006. *Harnessing knowledge dynamics: Principled organizational knowing & learning*. London: IRM Press.

Nonaka, I. 1994. A dynamic theory of organizational knowledge creation. *Organization Science*, 5(1), 14–37.

Nonaka, I. & Takeuchi, H. 1995. *The knowledge-creating company: How Japanese companies create the dynamics of innovation*. Oxford: Oxford University Press.

Nonaka, I. & Toyama, R. 2003. The knowledge-creating theory revisited: Knowledge creation as a synthetizing process. *Knowledge Management Research & Practice*, 1(1), 2–10.

Nonaka, I., Toyama, R. & Hirata, T. 2008. *Managing flow: A process theory of the knowledge-based firms*. Houndmills, UK: Palgrave Macmillan.

Nonaka, I. & Zhu, Z. 2012. *Pragmatic strategy: Eastern wisdom, global success*. Cambridge: Cambridge University Press.

North, K. & Kumta, G. 2018. *Knowledge management: Value creation through organizational learning*. 2nd edition. Cham: Springer.

Núñez, R. & Sweetser, E. 2006. With the future behind them: Convergent evidence from Aymara language and gesture in crosslinguistic comparison of spatial construals of time. *Cognitive Science*, 30, 401–50.

Nussbaum, M.C. 2001. *Upheavals of thought: The intelligence of emotions*. New York: Cambridge University Press.

O'Dell, C. & Hubert, C. 2011. *The new edge in knowledge: How knowledge management is changing the way we do business*. Hoboken, NJ: John Wiley & Sons.

Ohmae, K. 1982. *The mind of the strategist: The art of Japanese business*. New York: McGraw-Hill.

Örtenblad, A. 2011. *Making sense of the learning organization: What is it and who needs it?* Kuala Lumpur: Yayasan Ilmuwan.

Ouellet, M., Santiago, H., Israeli, Z. & Gabay, S. 2010. Is the future the right time? *Experimental Psychology*, 57(4), 308–14.

Parra, M. G., Nalda, A. L. & Peries, G. S. M. 2011. Towards a more humanistic understanding of organizational trust. *Journal of Management Development*, 30(6), 605–14.

Penrose, E. T. 1959. *The theory of the growth of the firm*. New York: John Wiley & Sons.

Penrose, E. T. 2013. *The theory of the growth of the firm*. Mansfield Centre, CT: Martino Publishing.

Pinker, S. 2008. *The stuff of thought: Language as a window into human nature*. New York: Penguin Books.

Polanyi, M. 1962. *Personal knowledge: Towards a post-critical philosophy*. Chicago: The University of Chicago Press.

Polanyi, M. 1983. *The tacit dimension*. Gloucester, MA: Peter Smith.

Porter, M. 1980. *Competitive strategy*. New York: Free Press.

Porter, M. 1985. *Competitive advantage: Creating and sustaining superior performance*. New York: Free Press.

Quinn, J. B. 1980. *Strategies for change: Logical incrementalism*. Homewood, IL: Irwin.

Raisch, S., Birkinshaw, J., Probst, G. & Tushman, M. L. 2009. Organizational ambidexterity: Balancing exploitation and exploration for sustained performance. *Organization Science*, 20(4), 685–95.

Reinholdt, M., Pederson, T. & Foss, N. J. 2011. Why a central network position isn't enough: The role of motivation and ability for knowledge sharing in employee networks. *Academy of Management Journal*, 54(6), 1277–99.

Rhem, A. J. 2017. *Knowledge management in practice*. Boca Raton, FL: CRC Press.

Ricceri, F. 2008. *Intellectual capital and knowledge management: Strategic management of knowledge resources*. London: Routledge.

Robbins, S. P. & DeCenzo, D. A. 2005. *Fundamentals of management: Essential concepts and applications*. 5th edition. London: Pearson/Prentice Hall.

Robinson, M. D., Watkins, E. R. & Harmon-Jones, E. (eds.). 2013. *Handbook of cognition and emotion*. New York: The Guilford Press.

Roth, A. V. 1996. Achieving strategic agility through economies of knowledge. *Planning Review*, 24(2), 30–6.

Rother, M. 2010. *Toyota kata: Managing people for improvement, adaptiveness, and superior results*. New York: McGraw-Hill.

Rousseau, D. M., Sitkin, S. B., Burt, R. S. & Camerer, C. 1998. Not so different after all: A cross-discipline view of trust. *Academy of Management Review*, 23(3), 393–404.

Rowley, J. 2007. The wisdom hierarchy: Representations of DIKW hierarchy. *Journal of Information Science*, 33(2), 163–80.

Rumelt, R. 2012. *Good strategy, bad strategy: The difference and why it matters*. London: Profile Books.

Rumsfeld, D. 2002. *Press conference at the U.S. Department of Defense*. Accessed January 10, 2014, from www.defense.gov/transcripts/transcript .aspx?transcriptid=2636.

Russell, B. 2009. *Human knowledge: Its scope and limits*. London: Routledge.

Ryle, G. 2002. *The concept of mind: With an introduction by Daniel C. Dennet*. Chicago: The University of Chicago Press.

Sanchez, J. H., Sanchez, Y. H., Collado-Tuiz, D. & Cebrian-Tarrason, D. 2013. Knowledge creating and sharing corporate culture framework. *Procedia: Social and Behavioral Sci*ences, 74, 388–97.

Santiago, J., Lupiañez, J., Pérez, E. & Funes, M. J. 2007. Time (also) flies from left to right. *Psychonomic Bulletin & Review*, 14(3), 512–16.

Schumpeter, J. A. 1950. *Capitalism, socialism, and democracy*. 3rd edition. New York: Harper & Row.

Segall, K. 2012. *Insane simple: The obsession that drives Apple's success*. London: Portfolio Penguin.

Seirafi, K. 2013. *Organizational epistemology: Understanding knowledge in organizations*. Heidelberg: Springer.

Senge, P. 1999. *The fifth discipline: The art and practice of the learning organization*. London: Random House.

Shannon, C. E. 1948. A mathematical theory of communication. *Bell System Technical Journal*, 27(3), 379–423.

Simon, H. A. 1979. Rational decision-making in business organizations. *The American Economic Review*, 69(4), 493–513.

Simon, H. A. 1987. Making management decisions: The role of intuition and emotion. *Academy of Management Executive*, 1(1), 57–64.

Simon, H. A. 1991. Organizations and markets. *Journal of Economic Perspectives*, 5, 25–44.

Simon, H. A. 2000. Bounded rationality in social sciences: Today and tomorrow. *Mind & Society*, 1, 25–39.

Sloan, A. P. 1963. *My years with General Motors*. London: Sedgewick & Jackson.

Snyman, R. & Kruger, C. J. 2004. The interdependency between strategic management and strategic knowledge management. *Journal of Knowledge Management*, 8(1), 5–19.

Song, J. & Lee, K. 2014. *The Samsung way: Transformational management strategies from the world leader in innovation and design*. New York: McGraw-Hill.

Spender, J.-C. 1996. Making knowledge the basis of a dynamic theory of the firm. *Strategic Management Journal*, 17, Special Issue, 45–62.

Spender, J.-C. 2003. Exploring uncertainty and emotion in the knowledge-based theory of the firm. *Information Technology & People*, 16 (3), 266–88.

Spender, J. -C. 2014. *Business strategy: Managing uncertainty, opportunity, & enterprise*. Oxford: Oxford University Press.

Spender, J.-C. 2015. The theory of managed firms (TMF). *Human Systems Management*, 34(1), 57–80.

Spender, J.-C. & Grant, R. M. 1996. Knowledge and the firm: Overview. *Strategic Management Journal*, 17, Special Issue, 5–9.

Spender, J.-C. & Strong, B. A. 2014. *Strategic conversations: Creating and directing the entrepreneurial workforce*. Cambridge: Cambridge University Press.

Stacey, R. D., Griffin, D. & Shaw, P. 2000. *Complexity and management: Fad or radical challenge to system thinking?* London: Routledge.

Stam, C. D. 2007. *Knowledge productivity: Designing and testing a method to diagnose knowledge productivity and plan for enhancement*. Twente, Netherlands: Twente University.

Stiglitz, J. E. & Walsh, C. E. 2002. *Economics*. New York: W.W. Norton & Company.

Sun Tzu. 1971. *The art of war*. New York: Oxford University Press.

Sutherland, S. 2013. *Irrationality: The enemy within*. London: Pinter & Martin.

Sveiby, K. E. 2001. A knowledge-base theory of the firm to guide in strategy formulation. *Journal of Intellectual Capital*, 2(4), 344–58.

Sveiby, K. E. 2010. Methods for measuring intangible assets. Online article. Accessed February 10, 2017, from www.sveiby.com/articles/intangibleMethods .htm.

Syrett, M. & Devine, M. 2012. *Managing uncertainty: Strategies for surviving and thriving in turbulent times*. London: Profile Books.

Szulanski, G. 1995. Unpacking stickiness: An empirical investigation of the barriers to transfer best practice inside the firm. *Academy of Management Proceedings*, August 1995, 437–41.

Szulanski, G. 1996. Exploring internal stickiness: Impediments to the transfer of best practice within the firm. *Strategic Management Journal*, 17, 27–43.

Szulanski, G. 2000. The process of knowledge transfer: A diachronic analysis of stickiness. *Organizational behavior and Human Decision Process*, 82(1), 9–27.

Szulanski, G. & Jensen, R. 2004. Overcoming stickiness: An empirical investigation of the role of the template in the replication of organizational routines. *Managerial and Decision Economics*, 25(67), 347–63.

Taleb, N. N. 2007. *The black swan: The impact of the highly improbable.* London: Penguin Books.

Taylor, F. W. 1998. *The principles of scientific management.* New York: Dover Publications.

Teece, D. J. 2009. *Dynamic capabilities and strategic management.* Oxford: Oxford University Press.

Tellis, G. J., Prabhu, J. C. & Chandy, R. K. 2009. Radical innovation across nations: The preeminence of corporate culture. *Journal of Marketing*, 73, 3–23.

Thatchenkery, T. 2005. *Appreciative sharing of knowledge: Leveraging knowledge management for strategic change.* Chagrin Falls, OH: Taos Institute Publications.

Thompson, Jr., A. A. & Strickland III, A. J. 2001. *Strategic management: Concepts and cases.* 12th edition. New York: McGraw-Hill Irwin.

Tichy, N. M. 1997. *The leadership engine: How winning companies build leaders at every level.* New York: Harper Business.

Tsai, W. 2001. Knowledge transfer in interorganizational networks: Effects of network position and absorptive capacity on business unit innovation and performance. *The Academy of Management Journal*, 44(5), 996–1004.

Tsoukas, H. 1996. The firm as a distributed knowledge system: A constructionist approach. *Strategic Management Journal*, 17, Special Issue, 11–25.

Vallejo-Alonso, B., Rodriguez-Castellanos, A. & Arregui-Ayastuy, G. 2011. *Identifying, measuring, and valuing knowledge-based intangible assets: New perspectives.* Hershey, PA: IGI Global.

Van der Heijden, K., Bradfield, R., Burt, G., Cairns, G. & Wright, G. 2002. *The sixth sense: Accelerating organizational learning with scenarios.* New York: John Wiley & Sons.

Van der Laan, L. & Yap, J. 2016. *Foresight & strategy in the Asia Pacific region: Practice and theory to build enterprises of the future.* Berlin: Springer.

Vanhala, M., Puumalainen, K. & Blomqvist, K. 2011. Impersonal trust: The development of the construct and the scale. *Personnel Review*, 40(4), 485–513.

Warren, K. 2008. *Strategic management dynamics.* New York: John Wiley & Sons.

Wellman, J. L. 2009. *Organizational learning: How companies and institutions manage and apply knowledge.* New York: Palgrave Macmillan.

Wenger, E. 1998. *Communities of practice: Learning, meaning, and identity.* New York: Cambridge University Press.

Wenger, E., McDermott, R. & Snyder, W. M. 2002. *A guide to managing knowledge: Cultivating communities of practice.* Boston, MA: Harvard Business School Press.

Wheelen, T. L. & Hunger, J. D. 2004. *Strategic management and business policy.* 9th edition. International edition. London: Prentice Hall.

Whittington, R. 2001. *What is strategy – and does it matter?* 2nd edition. London: Thomson Learning.

Wootton, S. & Horne, T. 2010. *Strategic thinking: A nine step approach to strategy and leadership for managers and marketers.* 3rd edition. London: Kogan Page.

Zack, M. H. 1999. Developing a knowledge strategy. *California Management Review,* 4(3), 125–45.

Zack, M. H. 2003. Rethinking the knowledge-based organization. *MIT Sloan Management Review,* 44(4), 67–71.

Zhou, R., Cai, R. & Tong, G. 2013. Applications of entropy in finance: A review. *Entropy,* 15, 4909–31.

Zieba, M. & Durst, S. 2018. Knowledge risks in the sharing economy. In Vatamanescu, E. M. & Pinzaru, F. (eds.). *Knowledge management sharing in the sharing economy.* Cham: Springer International Publishing, pp. 253–70.

Cambridge Elements ≡

Business Strategy

J.-C. Spender
Kozminski University

J.-C. Spender is a research Professor, Kozminski University. He has been active in the business strategy field since 1971 and is the author or co-author of 7 books and numerous papers. His principal academic interest is in knowledge-based theories of the private sector firm, and managing them.

About the Series
Business strategy's reach is vast, and important too since wherever there is business activity there is strategizing. As a field, strategy has a long history from medieval and colonial times to today's developed and developing economies. This series offers a place for interesting and illuminating research including industry and corporate studies, strategizing in service industries, the arts, the public sector, and the new forms of Internet-based commerce. It also covers today's expanding gamut of analytic techniques.

Cambridge Elements $\overline{\overline{}}$

Business Strategy

Elements in the Series

A full series listing is available at: www.cambridge.org/EBUS

Printed in the United States
by Baker & Taylor Publisher Services